Elusion Aforethought

Elusion Aforethought:
The Life and Writing
of Anthony Berkeley Cox

MALCOLM J. TURNBULL

Bowling Green State University Popular Press
Bowling Green, OH 43403

Library of Congress Cataloging-in-Publication Data
Turnbull, Malcolm J.
    Elusion aforethought : the life and writing of Anthony
Berkeley Cox / Malcolm J. Turnbull.
        p.   cm.
    Includes bibliographical references and index.
    ISBN 0-87972-715-2 (cloth). ISBN 0-87972-716-0 (pbk.)
    1. Berkeley, Anthony, 1893-1971. 2. Detective and mystery
stories, English--History and criticism. 3. Novelists, English--
20th century--Biography. 4. Satirists, English--20th century--
Biography. 5. Journalists--Great Britain--Biography.
I. Title.
PR6005.0855Z89   1996
823'.912--dc20
    [B]   96-25821
                                                                        CIP

Cover design by Gary Dumm

FOR JOHN AND SOLLY

CONTENTS

1

INTRODUCTION

Anthony Berkeley Cox was a popular and prolific English journalist, satirist and novelist in the period between the wars. His extensive written output encompassed a versatile mix of humorous sketches, comic operas, full-length fantasies and political analysis (under his own name), stage and radio plays, book reviews and (most enduringly) a series of skillful and literate detective stories. Many critics believe his finest achievements were two classic "inverted" crime novels, *Malice Aforethought* and *Before the Fact*, both published under the pseudonym Francis Iles. In his day, he was at least as well known under the name Anthony Berkeley, creator of Roger Sheringham, one of the more colorful sleuths in Golden Age detective fiction.

Cox has been called one of the most important and influential of Golden Age writers by such authorities as Haycraft, Symons and Keating. Yet he occupies a surprisingly ambivalent position in the history of the crime genre. To enthusiasts, he has attained cult status, and ranks among the all-time greats; otherwise he is a little-known and unjustly underrated figure. Just a fraction of his considerable output has been reprinted in the years since his death—or, indeed, since his heyday in the 1930s—and that only intermittently. *The Poisoned Chocolates Case, Trial and Error, Malice Aforethought* and *Before the Fact* are the only titles reissued with any frequency, and assessing Cox's overall written achievement is made more difficult by the extreme scarcity of some of his other books (crime or otherwise).[1] This, and the writer's preoccupation with anonymity, may account for the lack of critical attention he and his books have received. By contrast with the proliferation of biographical and critical analyses of Dorothy L. Sayers and Agatha Christie, for instance, the only detailed studies of Cox to date have been a chapter in LeRoy Panek's *Watteau's Shepherds* and articles by William Bradley Strickland, Melvyn Barnes and

Charles Shibuk.[2] Sayers and Cox were both born in 1893; significantly, Sayers's centenary was marked by a series of celebrations while Cox's anniversary seems to have passed largely unnoticed.

This book is a personal appreciation of Anthony Berkeley Cox's writing. Like the loving surveys of Agatha Christie's work compiled by Nancy Blue Wynne and Robert Barnard,[3] it grew out of my own intense enjoyment and enthusiasm for the Berkeley and Iles novels (and my fascination with the contradictory personality of their elusive author). My interest was first aroused by Julian Symons's laudatory assessment of *The Poisoned Chocolates Case* (in *Bloody Murder*).[4] Having read and fallen in love with that novel, I proceeded to track down as many of Cox's other detective novels and stories as I could, and in time, extended my search to include his noncrime publications. At different times my quest took me to secondhand bookstores as geographically dispersed as Melbourne, coastal California and Oxford. One fortunate visit to a mystery specialist in San Francisco netted four hard-to-find Sheringham books, while a mint copy of *Jugged Journalism* inexplicably surfaced in my rural hometown in Tasmania. Each acquisition confirmed my view that Cox was a uniquely talented individual, and a most unjustly neglected writer. On other occasions, my research into his life and work took me to university libraries in Melbourne, Honolulu and Cambridge, to Somerset House in London, Watford and rural Kent, while an undoubted highlight of the quest was reading the first edition of Cox's earliest novel, *The Layton Court Mystery*, in the reading room of the British Museum.

My study focuses primarily on Anthony Berkeley Cox's most lasting contribution to popular literature, that is, his skilled traditional murder-mysteries and "inverted" murder novels. At the same time however, I have been keen to examine the full range of the author's writing, including his comic novels, sketches, criticism and essays. Cox distinguished between his comic material, detective puzzles and studies of the criminal mind by employing a different pen name for each style, and I look at each publishing persona—A.B. Cox, Anthony Berkeley and Francis Iles—in turn. To obviate awkwardness or confusion over the pseudonyms, I have chosen to refer generally to the writer as ABC (rather than Cox, Berkeley Cox, etc.) and, where appropriate, as ABC/Berkeley or ABC/Iles. One chapter (on the Sheringham stories) has appeared in a different form in the journal *Clues*.[5] An additional chapter collates all the (admittedly limited) biographical detail available, while an appendix provides the interested reader with a chronological listing and capsule summary of ABC's major published works.

I should note here my indebtedness to two bibliographies—Paul R. Moy's modest listing in the *Armchair Detective* (most useful for details on the *Punch* sketches), and the much more comprehensive project undertaken by Ayresome Johns.[6] The latter is an essential reference tool for any ABC enthusiast or student; it is filled with pertinent and illuminating detail, including citations for a substantial body of unpublished material contained in a Berkeley Cox archive which was auctioned in London in 1992.[7] Also useful is Johns's highly informative introduction to the limited edition collection *The Roger Sheringham Stories*.[8]

At a personal level, I am indebted to several people: Professor W.D. (Bill) Rubinstein, of the University of Wales at Aberystwyth, for providing me with a copy of Johns's bibliography, and for alerting me to the writer's preoccupation with Edward VIII and the Simpson divorce; Marcia Harriman, a fellow ABC enthusiast, for her interest and comments on the study; and John Willis, for his valued assistance, and personal involvement (and perseverance), in the searching and researching process. I am particularly grateful to Celia Down, ABC's niece, and her husband, Norman, who cooperated fully, and who provided me with valuable insights into the writer's private life in the course of a wide-ranging interview.

2

Anthony Berkeley Cox (1893–1971)

Throughout his career, and up until his death, Anthony Berkeley Cox's fondness for mystery extended to his personal life. He avoided publicity (almost religiously) and actively delighted in camouflaging his real self behind pseudonyms, so keeping the public guessing as to the true identities of his alter egos. (Johns notes that he gleefully preserved press speculation about the writing talent behind the pen name Francis Iles.)[1] ABC seems to have been as much of an enigma to the public of the 1920s and 1930s as he is to a later generation. A studiously elusive man within a high-profile profession, his fetish for privacy and anonymity has always posed a considerable challenge to the would-be biographer, and a degree of guesswork must inevitably complement what few facts we have.[2]

He was born into the proverbial "comfortable circumstances" at 78 Queen's Road, Watford, Hertfordshire, on July 5, 1893. His father, Alfred Edward Cox (b. 1868), was a doctor (and son of a doctor) who hailed originally from Derbyshire; he gained a measure of fame late in life as inventor of a pioneering X-ray machine, which he used for locating shrapnel in patients during World War I. On his mother's side, ABC's lineage was somewhat more impressive: born at Watford in 1869, Sybil Maud Iles claimed descent from Robert Carey, Earl of Monmouth (d. 1639). Eight generations of the Iles family had occupied (and inherited) property which included two substantial adjoining buildings, Monmouth House and The Platts in Watford High Street, originally built by Carey as a dower-house.[3] According to an immensely detailed family tree on which ABC lavished a great deal of time and energy during his declining years, Sybil Iles's ancestors also included the celebrated botanist and illustrator Georg Dionysus Ehret[4] and Francis Iles, a notorious smuggler.

5

A cultivated and intellectually gifted woman, Sybil Iles was among the first generation of females to study at Oxford, in the years before the women's colleges were formally admitted into membership of the university. She subsequently ran a small private school in Watford prior to marrying Alfred Cox in 1891.[5] Perhaps ABC inherited his literary leanings from his mother; in 1905 she published a novel, *The School of Life: A Study in the Discipline of Circumstance.* There are obvious autobiographical elements in the book: Juliet, the heroine, studies at St Ursula's College, Oxford, becomes romantically smitten with a provincial physician (described as "handsome, well-read, clever and humorous, though somewhat cynical"), and earns her living as a schoolteacher before achieving wedded bliss at the fade-out. (She ends up marrying a steady vicar-*cum*-schoolmaster rather than the more dashing medico, however.) Rather tantalizingly, the novel makes reference to the town of Sheringham (Juliet holidays there), and a prominent character shoots himself behind locked doors (an already well-worn plot element which ABC would reprise—and adapt—in his first novel).[6]

ABC was the first of Alfred and Sybil Cox's three children. A daughter, Cynthia Cecily, was born in 1897 and a second son, Stephen Henry Johnson, in 1899. All three children were more than usually talented academically and artistically. Interestingly, ABC seems to have been the (relative) underachiever of the trio. He was educated at a day school in Watford and at Sherborne College, the ancient public school in Wessex. The *Sherborne Register* indicates that he was at the school from 1907 to 1911, and that he was a prefect, cadet sergeant and head of house there. He went on to University College, Oxford, where he managed only a Third in classics in 1914. The gifted Stephen, by contrast, won a scholarship to King's College, Cambridge, and earned honors as a mathematician; he ultimately spent many years as a schoolmaster in Kent. Like his brother, he contributed sketches to *Punch* in the 1920s, and also published several books (in Stephen's case, they were technical texts on algebra and trigonometry). Cynthia Cox obtained a doctorate in music in London, and was active in Oxford musical circles.[7]

In the absence of other detail on ABC's formative years, the Francis Iles opus *As for the Woman* provides us with some autobiographical insights. Celia Down, the writer's niece, has confirmed that the characters of Alan Littlewood, his mother and siblings, are family portraits; that being so, their interplay is revealing.[8]

Like Sybil Cox, Mrs Littlewood has been born and raised in a provincial town near London (Watford becomes Elmstead in the novel). She has studied at Oxford, has dabbled at teaching, and is the parent of a trio of talented children. Daughter Celia is a youthful professor of harmony at the Royal College of Music in London, while younger son Hugh is the envied recipient of a coveted science scholarship to Cambridge. Elder son Alan (that is, the author?), by comparison, has failed to match his robust siblings' heady intellectual and physical standards (he suffers from lung trouble, and has gone up to Oxford as a mere "commoner"). "If not the fool of a brilliant family," Alan is "at any rate the least brilliant member of it," and he is constantly intimidated by Celia and Hugh's attainments. Particularly galling to him is their failure to recognize that he may possess literary flair: "Celia and Hugh, Mrs. Littlewood too, for that matter, while never exactly setting themselves above him, all had a way of saying: 'Oh, well—Alan . . .' with a kind of affectionate depreciation which exasperated Alan extremely."[9]

Alan's first venture into print is a sonnet published in a popular magazine. The young man glows with satisfaction at being able to present the published work to his family, and the reader shares his anguish when he inadvertently overhears his mother dismiss the sonnet as "empty, pretentious nonsense."[10] According to Johns, ABC's first published work was also a romantic 14-line poem (of limited appeal). Titled "To Evadne," it appeared anonymously in the *Grand Magazine* in September 1913:

> Cupid hides his eyes in shame,
> Venus shades her beauty's flame.
> Cupid's gloomy! Venus cross!
> They in turn bemoan their loss.
> "I was God of Love", says Cupid.
> Venus says, "Don't be so stupid;
> My complaint is greater far, -
> I was beauty's brightest star!

> Now one little mortal maid
> Makes our heavenly glories fade.
> Fairer is she far than I" -
> Cupid heaves a plaintive sigh, -
> "Yes, and in her eyes alone
> Shines more love than I have known".[11]

We can only guess how far Sybil Cox's response to "To Evadne" anticipated Mrs Littlewood.

Any aspirations ABC may have had to gain recognition as a poet were necessarily put on hold with the outbreak of the Great War. He enlisted, attained the rank of lieutenant with the 7th Northumberland Regiment, was gassed in France, and invalided out with his health permanently impaired. Details of his professional life in the immediate postwar years are a little vague. Returning to civilian life in 1918, he apparently spent time in a succession of occupations, including "social work," work "in a Government office" (his descriptions), and real-estate dealings.[12] We know that he maintained a professional address off the Strand in London, that he was a director of Publicity Services Ltd., advertising specialists, for some years, and that he was one of two directors of the firm A.B. Cox Ltd. According to Celia Down, he never worked full time after the war, most of his time and energy being devoted to managing and overseeing family properties, and increasingly—as the 1920s progressed—to writing. We know that he resented being forced to pay the "excessive taxes" due on his combined incomes in the 1930s.[13]

It is not generally known that ABC married twice. His first wife was Margaret Fearnley Farrar (b. 1898); they wed while he was on leave in London in December 1917. Margaret Cox is the dedicatee of *The Professor on Paws* and *Malice Aforethought*, and we also know that she was involved with her husband in his amateur theatrical activities at Watford. (She designed the women's costumes for the stage version of *The Family Witch*, for instance.) The couple divorced in 1931, and Margaret Cox subsequently married Kenneth Nielsen, the man cited as her co-respondent in the court action. ABC's pointed references to Great Britain's "immoral and antiquated divorce laws" in the polemic *O England* (1934) suggest that the parting was amicable. Kenneth Nielsen publicly endorsed the writer's comments on book reviewing a couple of years later, and ABC remained on sufficiently good terms with his ex-wife to endow her with 1,000 pounds in his will. (Margaret Nielsen died in 1973.)[14]

In 1932 he married Helen Peters (nee MacGregor), former wife of his literary agent, A.D. Peters. No children were born of either of the Cox unions although Helen brought her two children by Peters with her. (We have no information on ABC's relations with his step-children.) The marriage itself broke down by the late 1940s, and the parting again appears to have been reasonably friendly: Helen Cox moved out of the couple's London flat into one on the floor below, and continued to provide her husband with some domestic services (including washing his clothes). Divorce proceedings were never instituted; Helen Cox predeceased her husband by several years.[15]

Again, ABC's writing may shed some light on his marital track record. References in the novels and *O England* indicate that he was nothing if not conservative in his attitude to women. One cringes today at some of his statements that imply a deep-rooted bitterness and a marked misogyny. "I am not a feminist," he once declared. "I am, if anything . . . a masculinist. I believe that, on balance, the typical masculine qualities are more use to the community as a community than the typically feminine ones."[16] Although a feature of ABC's prescription for healing the ailments afflicting British society was active involvement of women in government, he displayed an unenlightened perception of female capacity. (Women were much too prone to "take sides" and overly preoccupied with human relationships, he sniffed.) In *Jumping Jenny*, ABC seems to accord with the view that the irritating female victim needed to be married to "a great big he-man who'd give her a sound thrashing every now and then."[17] In *The Wychford Poisoning Case*, women are termed "adorable idiots," who live entirely by their emotions and are "fundamentally incapable of reason."[18] Given *Malice Aforethought*'s relentlessly jaundiced delineation of its female characters, and the distinctly unsympathetic nature of the wife, could there have been deliberate irony (or black humor) in the fact that ABC dedicated the book to his first wife? (Only a year later, *Before the Fact* was dedicated to Wife No. 2.)

The poem "To Evadne" is the only pre-1920s work by the writer to surface to date.[19] His professional writing career appears to have commenced in earnest in 1922 with the first of some 250 light, often satiric, sketches for *Punch, The Humorist, London Opinion, The Passing Show,* and other popular journals. A number of these sketches were subsequently collected in book form: a series which detailed the activities of an irrepressible little girl (something of a female variation on the Richmal Crompton character "William") reappeared as *Brenda Entertains,* while a group of "lessons" on fiction-writing for *Punch* was republished as *Jugged Journalism.* ABC apparently intended to collect and reprint many more of his humorous sketches and romantic short stories in book form (under the titles *Down Our Road, Cash on Delivery* and *Crimes of the Times and Other Misdemeanours*) but these projects never got beyond the planning stage.[20] In a similar (comic) vein, ABC published two full-length whimsical fantasies in the 1920s, *The Professor on Paws* and *The Family Witch,* both of which are reminiscent of P.G. Wodehouse. *The Family Witch* started life as a comic opera, mounted and staged by an amateur theatrical troupe called the Gnats in 1924; ABC displayed his versatility by providing both book and score, and enacting the part of the butler.[21] Later in the decade, he collaborated with composer J.J. Sterling Hill in another, Gilbert and Sullivan–style musical fantasy; following its Watford premiere, "The Merchant Prince" enjoyed a brief London season.[22]

In an early contribution to *Punch,* ABC observed that the detective story was just about the only variety of fiction for which there seemed to be a good market, and he resolved to try his hand at the form.[23] He was also motivated by his personal fondness for a genre which had only recently entered what we now recognize was its Golden Age.

The English detective story—pioneered by Sir Arthur Conan Doyle (with Sherlock Holmes), and nurtured by such practitioners as Baroness Orczy (The Old Man in the Corner), R. Austin Freeman (Dr Thorndyke), A.E.W. Mason (Inspector Hanaud) and G.K. Chesterton (Father Brown)—attained maturity and came into its own in the period between the wars. Robert Graves notes that it dominated popular reading at the time. Its immense popularity was aided by technological advances in publishing and advertising which, for the first time, combined to market large quantities of cheap books to a rapidly expanding readership.[24] Robert Barnard argues that the detective story and novel provided an escapist diversion for a British public devastated by the loss of three quarters of a million of its youth in the Great War, in much the same way that Restoration comedy had succeeded the traumas of the Civil War and Protectorate.

In 1920 the English middle classes had seen empires crumble, new Bolshevik republics established, Labour parties flourishing, a whole battalion of middle class standards collapse. They suspected, like the Restoration nobility, that their world was gone forever, and they took refuge in a form of literature that was hedged with rules and conventions, that flourished on stereotyped situations and characters, that looked back to a period of stability . . .[25]

Golden Age detective novels, or "whodunits," enshrined a set ritual: crime, investigation, deduction and solution. Populated with stock, one-dimensional characters, usually presided over by omniscient detecting superhumans (successors to the infallible Holmes), they were consciously devised as intellectual puzzles, elaborate games to be played out between author and reader according to stylized principles. LeRoy Panek maintains that English crime-writers of the period "participated in a literary movement which was as conscious and definable as the well-known movements in regular literature"; as befitting a movement, many of them regularly traded hypotheses, jokes and plot suggestions, and this camaraderie later prompted ABC to found and organize the Detection Club.[26] The "school" encompassed scores of writers, from plodding hacks of little lasting talent, through to the intelligent—and, in a few cases, gifted—craftspeople whose work remains popular and widely read today. Freeman Wills Crofts, Margery Allingham, Father Ronald Knox, J.S. Fletcher, John Rhode, Herbert Adams, G.D.H. and Margaret Cole, H.C. Bailey, Henry Wade, Anthony Gilbert, Milward Kennedy (and slightly later, Ngaio Marsh, Cyril Hare, Michael Innes and Nicholas Blake) were among the more prominent. Arguably at the head of the school were Dorothy L. Sayers, whose scholarly analyses of the evolution of crime fiction gave the form a degree of literary legitimacy, and the prolific Agatha Christie.[27] (ABC himself acknowledged Christie's primacy on more than one occasion.)[28]

Julian Symons ranks ABC's achievements in the field with those of Sayers and Christie, an assessment with which most of his devotees (myself included) heartily concur.[29] His first detective story (and first novel), *The Layton Court Mystery*, was issued anonymously in 1925; its popularity persuaded the writer to focus most of his creative energy into crime in the future (although he continued to explore other literary avenues on occasion). Between 1925 and 1939, ABC published 14 full-length detective stories under the pen name Anthony Berkeley, 10 of which featured his unconventional and spectacularly fallible amateur sleuth, Roger Sheringham. ABC endowed Sheringham with an upper-middle-class background and biographical details very similar to his own; also a writer, Sheringham echoed many of ABC's own attitudes and opinions on British society between the wars, although the personalities of creator and character diverged dramatically. A second amateur sleuth, the timid but remarkably astute Ambrose Chitterwick, seems to have been more of a self-portrait. Mr Chitterwick stole the limelight from Sheringham in *The Poisoned Chocolates Case*, and then starred in two cases of his own.

As well as the Berkeley novels, ABC published two comic crime exercises under his real name (A.B. Cox), *Mr Priestley's Problem* and *The Wintringham Mystery*. The latter was written for serialization in the *Daily Mirror*; a revised version appeared as *Cicely Disappears* (by the pseudonymous A. Monmouth Platts) in 1927. Most historians of the Golden Age believe that the writer's major achievements were the first two of the three "inverted" novels he wrote under the name Francis Iles; both *Malice Aforethought* and *Before the Fact* are generally regarded as masterpieces and decisive influences on postwar detective realism in Britain. Also influential, albeit at a more mundane level, was ABC's creation of the Detection Club in 1928, in conjunction with Dorothy L. Sayers. A social and intellectual/ideological meeting-ground for almost all the leading practitioners of the genre, the Detection Club produced a number of collaborative publishing and broadcasting ventures and, in a partly tongue-in-cheek gesture, formulated a "fair play" code which ordained what was and was not orthodox in authors' competitions to fool or tantalize their readers via the puzzle-story. ABC satirized the club as the Crime Circle (in *The Poisoned Chocolates Case*), and he gleefully deviated from its code of practice on a number of occasions, but the organization's existence was a testament to his extreme enthusiasm for that type of fiction, and he retained associations with the club for many years.

The writer lived at West Bromley in Kent and at Watford in the immediate period after World War I. With success, he acquired a fashionable London address, a flat at 86 Hamilton Terrace, St John's Wood; an agreement with Lady Hore (of the banking family) enabled him to occupy the top floor of the building rent free for his lifetime, on the understanding that it reverted to the Hore family after his death. In 1930 he purchased a country retreat called Linton Hills, near the village of Welcombe Bideford on the Devon/Cornwall border. The term *country retreat* implies a cottage; in fact, Linton Hills was/is set in 100 acres of inaccessible forest land. Originally a cluster of three cottages, the dwelling was remodeled and expanded substantially by ABC who (his niece recalls) quarried his own stone for the reconstruction work. Although rather damp, dark and uncompromisingly "basic" during his lifetime, the remodeled structure had "splendid potential." ABC spent lengthy periods there and his cousin, Cyril Ehret Iles, took over and modernized the property in the 1970s. (Linton Hills remained in the family until quite recently.)[30]

ABC had a particular affection for Monmouth House in Watford, which he inherited during the interwar years. In his will, he expressed the hope that his trustees would retain the property for as long as possible (in view of the length of time it had been owned by members of the Iles dynasty). Shares in the building were distributed among his brother's children and other relatives after his death.[31] Monmouth House remains prominent in Watford's High Street, although redevelopment of the town's bustling business center has entailed extensive renovation; in the 1990s, its ground floor houses clothing and furniture stores. (ABC's birthplace, in nearby Queen's Road, now houses a car alarm and audio shop.)

The variety of ABC's written output reflected the man's personal complexity. As well as the comic novels, musical fantasies and satirical sketches he published under his own name, and the Berkeley and Iles stories and novels, he authored several unpublished stage and radio plays and wrote a number of undistinguished popular songs. In a more serious vein, he issued a deeply felt critique of 1930s Britain in *O England*. His last published novel was *As for the Woman* (1939) by Francis Iles. For the next 30 years, apart from a couple of short stories printed in the early 1940s but written earlier (and two negligible—and self-indulgent—collections of limericks), his published output was limited to book reviews for the *Sunday Times* (intermittently after World War II, and regularly from 1953 to 1956) and the *Manchester Guardian* (from 1956 to 1970). He maintained his association with the Detection Club, however, and also hosted meetings of the crime critical fraternity at his Hamilton Terrace flat.

We can only speculate on the reasons behind ABC's decision to stop writing fiction after 1939. A number of theories have been put forward. In view of the intensity of his diatribes against English taxation (in *O England*), it is likely that he found most of the profits from his writing swallowed up by the Government. Sizeable legacies, including Monmouth House and another property, Westerham, had left him without the need to earn his living; no doubt, Hollywood deals for the picture rights to two of his novels (*Trial and Error* and *Before the Fact*, filmed as *Flight from Destiny* and *Suspicion* respectively) also contributed to his financial independence, and he found that compiling review columns paid handsomely. (Very early in his career, he had insisted that he would happily stop writing crime fiction once he discovered something more lucrative.)[32] At his death, his estate was estimated at an enviable 178,035 pounds net.[33]

There were probably other factors. Certainly he had domestic difficulties. Relations with his brother and sister were "distant" (at best) at this time because of conflict with them over his having inherited (or bought out) much of the Iles property.[34] It is likely, also, that marriage problems had some impact. ABC once told John Dickson Carr that he wrote *As for the Woman* during a period of severe emotional strain; the book's lack of critical and commercial success affected him deeply, causing him to lose interest, and he steadfastly resisted all persuasion to continue writing.[35] Two Francis Iles follow-ups (a sequel to *As for the Woman* and a novel dealing with perceived inequities in the jury system) were advertised but never appeared.[36]

Clearly ABC must have been working under some pressure in the 1930s. His written and spoken statements evidence his profound dissatisfaction with the sociopolitical status quo, and hint at an even deeper personal turmoil. An irresistible wave of anger with English law and politics impelled him to publish *O England* in 1934.[37] Three years later, his refusal to pay a motoring fine, and a resultant court appearance, made the papers. Ordered to pay 30 shillings for failing to observe a halt sign, ABC declared he would sooner go to jail than do so. (In his view—as an experienced motorist of 26 years—it would have been more dangerous to have stopped than to have slowed down at the intersection in question.) The magistrate, Lord Carrington, had little sympathy with his argument, and censured the writer: "There are many things in this world that I and everybody else in this court do not agree with, but if everybody took your attitude life would be chaos."[38] Presumably ABC ultimately thought better of the matter and paid the fine. He did sublimate some of his annoyance into an unpublished short story, "It Isn't Fair." In the story, a man convicted of a minor driving offense leaves the courthouse in a rage. His anger causes him to crash into the car of the policeman who originally booked him. The policeman's car is parked on the blind side of a bend.[39]

In the same period, the writer took another, very controversial stand on a matter of principle—a stand which now seems to have bordered on the irrational. Intensely disturbed over Edward VIII's abdication, and convinced that the king should be saved from himself, ABC reportedly spent a fortune on lawyers and private detectives in a quest to find "bedroom evidence" of adultery between Edward and Mrs Simpson. He obviously hoped thus to compromise Mrs Simpson's *decree nisi* and so prevent her remarriage. ABC offered to provide the King's Proctor with witnesses recruited from a Budapest hotel, provided that their travelling expenses could be reimbursed.

Edward VIII's biographer, Philip Ziegler, maintains that none of ABC's evidence would have stood up in court, and that an embarrassed Proctor indicated that no funds were available for such a purpose (nor would it be proper to pay witnesses to give evidence). Interestingly, ABC's stand was not unique. A solicitor's clerk alleged publicly that the Simpson divorce had been founded on collusion and so could not be rendered absolute, and there were reports of a conspiracy among "certain young hotheads" in the military "to take up arms against the Government and for the King." ABC's detailed journal of his proceedings is now held at the Royal Archives, Windsor, and a carbon copy was offered for auction at Sotheby's in February 1993.[40]

ABC was (and remains) a singularly elusive and enigmatic figure, complex and contradictory; his light touch as a writer of fiction contrasts markedly with the intense anger implicit in passages in the novels and his public actions, and this duality characterized his personal life. Howard Haycraft described him as a "delightful and witty correspondent" and a genial host in the 1930s. James Sandoe, who met the ailing writer when he was touring the United States by bus around 1960, found him charming ("his heart was weak but his spirit gallant"). Christianna Brand knew him well, and once assessed him as "an excellent companion, clever, erudite, and very well read" (perhaps the cleverest of all the Detection Club members). Julian Symons, who was acquainted with ABC for 20 years, has remembered that he could be "a most engaging companion, particularly sympathetic to the young."[41] Celia Down got to know her uncle in her late teens, following his belated reconciliation with her father (Stephen Cox); in her view, ABC was attracted by her youth. In the late 1940s, he treated her to a holiday/rest-cure to Madeira and the Canary Islands, and played host to her regularly in London and Devon over the next two decades. She retains fond and vivid memories of accompanying him to the annual dinner of the Detection Club on the night that Ngaio Marsh was inducted, and recalls his enjoyment of the proceedings (as well as the presence there of Christie and Sayers).[42] ABC's book reviews testify to his encouragement of young writers and such newcomers to the detective field as Ianthe Jerrold.[43]

Yet, as notably generous as he could be with praise (and money) on the right occasion, ABC could be extraordinarily stingy over trifles. "I have known him to go to some trouble to avoid buying a drink for a man he disliked," recalls Symons. "Unpredictable as a person" (according to John Dickson Carr's widow, Clarice), intimidating, imperious, sometimes even "a bit frightening" (according to Norman Down), "touchy and crotchety when he felt his dignity was called into question" (according to Symons), ABC once resigned from the circle of critics who picked the best crime story of the year at an annual luncheon because he disagreed violently with one particular choice. He resigned similarly from the Detection Club, possibly because—as founder—he felt he (and not Agatha Christie) should have been elected president after Dorothy L. Sayers's death.[44]

He appears to have become more and more of an eccentric as the years passed. Diffident on one hand about his own well-crafted crime novels, and skeptical about any lasting importance he might have in the history of the genre, on the other he would insist on inflicting copies of his substandard collections of limericks on his circle of acquaintances ("he expected not merely acknowledgement of them but also words of praise").[45] His will contains the telling directive to his trustees that they employ doctors to ensure he is really dead, so as to avoid being buried alive—shades of Edgar Allan Poe! (As it happened, he would die in hospital.)[46] A persistent sufferer with asthma in his later years, he was apt "to disconcert anybody carrying on a conversation with him by suddenly placing a mask over his face, pumping away at a little rubber bulb and then taking deep breaths." Symons suggests that this mask was both real and symbolic, and that something "disturbingly shy and secretive" may well have been disguised by ABC's "ruddy-faced geniality."[47] When a rusty nail once appeared mysteriously in ABC's soup at a literary luncheon, Symons found himself unable to decide whether it could have been placed there by a careless cook, an offended author, or the writer himself. ("With Anthony Berkeley Cox such a joke was possible.")[48]

Inclination and ill-health (in addition to ongoing respiratory ailments, he was plagued with diabetes, circulation problems and severe bloating as a result of drug therapy) made the writer a recluse in his final years—"a bit run to seed and degenerating into sick miserliness—hoarding his considerable wealth."[49] His disillusionment with British bureaucracy and government did not lessen with the years, and he delighted in trying to outwit the Inland Revenue, secreting cash under floorboards and stowing silver in false cupboards at Linton Hills. The Devon house also provided storage space for piles of old magazines, masses of grocers' books and household accounts, and a sizeable stock of homemade wines (including his own raspberry concoction). A keen philatelist, he invested in collections of stamps, buying them up in bulk in the hope their market value would increase; some of his acquisitions did prove profitable, but one purchase—several crates of Victory stamps—bombed badly. (The Victory issues were produced in such large quantities that any return on them was negligible.) Generous as he could be on the right occasion, ABC was extraordinarily penny-pinching with himself, relying on a "dreadful old car," rarely providing himself with new clothes and preferring to keep his homes "freezing cold" rather than pay "unnecessary" heating bills. The Linton Hills property remained without electricity in his lifetime (notwithstanding its primitive facilities though, the "squire" always dressed formally for dinner there and expected his guests to do likewise). He had few friends and saw them less and less as the years passed. At the same time, he seems to have inspired considerable loyalty in his employees. A string of London housekeepers reportedly "doted" on him, and he was very highly regarded by the long-serving caretaker at Linton Hills.[50]

Norman Down remembers that ABC remained surprisingly philosophical about his rapidly deteriorating health in his final months, and that "he knew when to go." His last professional task was the Criminal Records column for the *Manchester Guardian* in September 1970. He died at St Mary's Hospital, Paddington, on March 9, 1971, the cause of death specified as a combination of pneumonia, chronic bronchitis and congestive cardiac failure. His name was recorded erroneously on the death certificate as Anthony *Beverley* Cox.[51] (Obituaries appeared in the major British newspapers and *Ellery Queen's Mystery Magazine*.)[52] His will stipulated that he be buried with other members of his family in the Vicarage Road Cemetery at Watford, and although he once confided to Christianna Brand that "there was not one soul in the world he did not cordially dislike," he had ensured that his extensive estate benefited relatives, friends and former employees. His literary copyrights, royalties and shares in A.B. Cox Ltd. were bequeathed to the Society of Authors, Playwrights and Composers.[53]

Although there has been some renewed interest in ABC's work in the two decades since he died, and several of his crime novels have been reprinted (at infrequent intervals), little recognition has been accorded the full range of his achievement in his three literary guises. In the following chapters, I will examine his output in each persona, as Cox, Berkeley and Iles.

3

A.B. Cox, Humorist

Sketches

When pressed for a few biographical details by Howard Haycraft in 1939, ABC noted that he began his writing career with sketches for *Punch,* "a so-called humorous periodical peculiar to this country."[1] Thanks to Paul R. Moy's detective work, we know that he contributed some 60 humorous pieces to that famous journal, starting with "The Brown Berry" in November 1922, and finishing with "Rosamund Regained" in March 1929.[2] Die-hard enthusiasts have always assumed that *Punch* was only one of the magazines ABC wrote for in the 1920s, but it was not until Ayresome Johns catalogued the writer's own scrapbook recently that we were made aware of the full extent of his noncrime publications. "I Wonder" appears to have been his first magazine sketch (a husband and wife are caught out inadvertently flirting with each other at a masked ball); it appeared in the *Democrat* 9 Sept. 1922. ABC subsequently supplied nearly 200 more sketches and skits to *London Opinion, The Humorist, Tit-Bits, Happy Mag, The Westminster Weekly Gazette, The Passing Show, The Blue, Green, Sovereign* and *Grand* magazines, *Pan, George Robey's Christmas Annual,* and others.

Periodicals of this kind thrived in pre-World War II England, and provided a livelihood for scores of journalists. As ABC observed on one occasion: "This is the magazine age. Every month or two a new magazine unfolds its leaves and bursts in full bloom upon an eager public like some delicate flower."[3] All except *Punch* have long since disappeared, however, and issues of many of them are now very rare. Some of the author's contributions to them are anonymous (we know they are his only because he preserved copies of them); some bear the initials A.B.C., and others are bylined A.B. Cox. The majority of the pieces were composed between 1923 and 1926, by which time he was gaining a reputation as a novelist. (ABC contributed only two sketches to *Punch* after 1926, for instance.) A few representative samples can give us a general idea of their style and content.

In a short series collectively titled "If They'd Done It," for *Passing Show,* nursery rhymes were retold "as they might have been written" by P.G. Wodehouse, Sir Arthur Conan Doyle, H.G. Wells, W.W. Jacobs or A.S.M. Hutchinson. "Oxford Reborn" (*Passing Show* 2 June 1923) humorously speculates on that university's future should the unthinkable happen and extracurricular activities be outlawed in favor of scholarly pursuits! "The Sweets of Triumph" (*Passing Show* 23 Dec. 1924) offers a tantalizing foretaste of a later triumph: the well-publicized arrival of a box of poisoned chocolates effectively speeds up sales of a struggling author's book. "A Lesson in Tact" (*Punch* 27 Feb. 1924) fantasizes about the topical practice of grafting monkey glands onto humans (as a rejuvenating agent). "Legislation by Threats" (*Passing Show* 28 April 1923) and "Fine Distinctions" (*Punch* 14 March 1924) underline the author's cynical estimate of professional politics and politicians. "Spats and Perdition" (*Punch* 6 Aug. 1924) is a very funny, Wodehousian account of the debilitating effect wearing spats might have on the strong, silent "he-man" of romantic fiction. "Life with the Gloves Off" (*Blue Magazine* Oct. 1924), "Convincing Mona" (*Tit-Bits* 22 Dec. 1923) and "Tea at the Cottage" (*Happy Mag* March 1924) are standard lightweight love stories. "A Story Against Reviewers" (*Punch* 3 June 1925) is a heartfelt dig at serious novelists and so-called professional critics: a soul-searching novel called *Anaesthesia* is mistakenly sent out to reviewers as a detective story—with ludicrous results. (ABC confided that this sketch had been inspired by "recent regrettable experiences.") "What They're Thinking" (*Passing Show* 20 Jan. 1923) details ABC's musings about his fellow passengers on a London bus. In "Love and the Car" (*London Opinion* 13 Dec. 1924), a young man becomes infatuated with his new automobile. "The Right to Kill" (*Democrat* 30 Dec. 1922) is an early departure from the comic mode: an anesthetist is uncertain what action to take when a drugged patient starts talking in loving terms about the anesthetist's wife. A chance remark by an eminent surgeon saves the patient's life. (John calls the story the first published hint of ABC's Francis Iles Persona.)[4]

The A.B. Cox sketches and skits satirized or commented wryly on a broad range of contemporary fads and issues, from university courses in "Truth-telling" to the difficulty of obtaining a refund on an unused railway ticket or the virtues of condensed milk. A large proportion of them can be classified in series: some 50 sketches featured a formidable little girl named Brenda, while many others described domestic and social events amongst a set of recurring characters in a semirural community. ABC revised some of the Brenda stories for his first book, *Brenda Entertains*. A series of sketches on short-story writing, which he contributed to *Punch* in 1924, resurfaced as *Jugged Journalism* the following year, and ABC also played with the idea of collecting many of his other sketches and romantic stories in book form.

The little girl who was to become Brenda was introduced in "The Brown Berry," ABC's first contribution to *Punch*. At that stage, she was called Margaret; she appeared in another two *Punch* sketches, "The Church Mouse" and "The Grig," before the author changed her name and transferred her exploits to *The Humorist*.[5] In all, the collection *Brenda Entertains*, published by humor specialist Herbert Jenkins in January 1925, brings together 27 stories, most of them reprints from the two magazines. It seems likely that the immense success of Richmal Crompton's stories featuring the unquenchable 11-year-old William Brown influenced ABC's choice of character. Brenda is a self-possessed young lady of seven who, like William, plagues her family and their friends with her unquenchable thirst for knowledge. The family has learned by experience to head Brenda away from potentially knotty queries or to give her more or less convincing replies (hoping, in that way, to keep her quiet until they have time to look the subject up). Thus her chief victim becomes her elder sister's mild-mannered beau, Mr Smith, a medical student and aspiring writer.[6]

Brenda tyrannizes over Mr Smith, constantly testing his ingenuity with questions like "What is a welkin?" "Why don't you wear stays?" "Why does the wind blow?" "What's a grig?" "What's a trivet?". While Smith secretly suspects that the child might not respect him much, he is loath to lose what little advantage he has by ever confessing his ignorance; he is also acutely aware that any admission of failure might lower his beloved's regard for him. His compliance lands him in a sequence of embarrassing predicaments: on one occasion, he mistakenly pounces on the vicar's wife after being coerced by Brenda into a game of lions. Enlisted to help her in the garden, he inadvertently throws away all the seedlings and plants lines of weeds. He goes for a walk with Brenda and finds himself alone in a field with a bull. When he threatens to chastise her following a particularly uncomfortable encounter, she totally disarms him by announcing she would like to be spanked (just to find out what it feels like). All ends happily, of course; the final chapter finds Brenda acting as matchmaker to Smith and her sister.

Brenda Entertains was a pleasant, if unremarkable, first book; that same year ABC followed it up with his first detective story, *The Layton Court Mystery* (see chapter 4), and a second Cox opus, *Jugged Journalism*. He did not abandon his Brenda character and, in fact, furnished *The Humorist* with two dozen more stories about her over the next couple of years.[7]

Jugged Journalism is easily the best of the A.B. Cox books, and is notable for including several clever parodies of mystery/detective stories. Published by Herbert Jenkins, the book consists of 20 (often deliciously) tongue-in-cheek lessons on the art of short-story writing, with examples to illustrate each story type. ABC examines in turn the simple love tale; detective, mystery, gruesome and tense stories; nature, children's, business and strong-man tales; essays, newspaper work and verse; literary style and the practical aspects of getting written work published. Twelve of the lessons are revised reprints of the *Punch* originals, and the rest draw on other material previously published in *Punch, The Passing Show* and *The Humorist*. Highlights of *Jugged Journalism* are its 32 illustrations by cartoonist George Morrow, including an oft-reprinted caricature of ABC as the frontispiece. The popular authors satirized in the examples include Wodehouse, Edgar Wallace, Ethel M. Dell and A.S.M. Hutchinson. One short skit, the charming recipe for a "model story," is worth repeating here for its distinctively Coxian humor.

In line with ABC's emphasis on the importance of starting off any story with a trenchant remark: "Sir James McGrisgsby raised the pistol with a quivering hand, and pointed it full in his daughter's face." From there (notes ABC), the action of the story should build the reader up to a "fever-pitch of excitement":

'Stop father!' screamed the girl. 'Stop, before you do anything you may be sorry for.'

Sir James' face, dusky red with suppressed emotion, took on a more purple tinge. He strove to speak, but the strangled sounds that issued from his lips bore no resemblance to words.

Then, suddenly, his finger tightened convulsively on the trigger. There was a sob and a scream, and the weapon discharged its contents straight into the face of the shrieking girl.

Finally: the denouement (which is an early confirmation of the author's delight in the unexpected).

'Got you that time!' exploded the baronet, almost speechless with laughter, his finger still clasping the trigger of the water-pistol. 'That'll teach you to drench me when I'm asleep.'

'But I told you you'd be sorry, father, and so you will,' laughed the girl, wiping the water from her face. 'You've simply ruined this frock, and you'll jolly well have to buy another!'[8]

Jugged Journalism makes effective use of the diversity of ABC's skits and sketches, and Johns notes that the writer planned to collect a large number of his other short pieces in three more collections, none of which ever appeared. *Cash on Delivery* was to consist of 16 short stories; although mostly straight romances, ABC also intended to include a ghost story ("The Green Dress"), the forerunner of his novel *Mr Priestley's Problem,* and a couple of immature efforts which anticipate his Francis Iles persona ("The Benefit of the Doubt" and "The Man Who Could Hear"). *Crimes of the Times and Other Misdemeanours* (which, notwithstanding the title, would have been of no detective interest) was a proposed general miscellany of published and unpublished sketches and short stories. A more cohesive project was a compendium to be called *Down Our Road: A Record of Everyday Things,* in which ABC planned to formalize an extensive series of loosely connected sketches which detailed the activities of a rural social network. Johns notes that a typescript exists of an opening chapter in which a comic writer and his wife arrive in the village of Horsley in Kent.[9] Recurring characters include Miss Porter, the local social arbiter, and several couples, most notably the Cox-like George and Marion.

Typical of the *Down Our Road* sketches are "The Deturfers" (*Punch* 7 March 1923) and an unpublished companion-piece, "The Levellers," which detail the aggravations faced by George and Marion and a second couple, Henry and Anne, in attempting to convert a small field into a fashionable tennis court. In "The Author's Crowning Hour" (*Punch* 29 Oct. 1924), George's excitement at lunching with the prospective publisher of his first book is dampened by his wife's mild skepticism. She fails to appreciate the effort involved when he sets out to compose a hit jingle in "My Popular Song" (*Humorist* 7 March 1925), and she transgresses the unwritten law in "Detective Marion" (*London Opinion* 25 July 1925), by revealing "whodunit" before George has a chance to finish reading the latest detective story. George and Marion debate the difficulties of ensuring regular hot baths in the country in "Hot Water" (*Punch* 14 May 1924), while in "A Dressy Affair" (*Punch* 24 Sept. 1924), Marion's inability to decide what dress to wear to a dinner-party inspires her husband to exhibit similar indecisiveness about the merits of tails over dinner-jacket, or pearl studs over gold ones.[10]

Comic Novels

ABC wrote four comic novels—two fantasies and two crime burlesques—as A.B. Cox. The first of these, *The Family Witch: An Essay in Absurdity* (1926) was a novelization of an earlier creation, a two-act comic opera of the same name, written and composed by the author in 1924. "The Family Witch" was staged by the Gnats in aid of the Watford and District Peace Memorial Hospital. ABC and his first wife were both involved in the production, and he played the role of the Major-Domo.[11] The novel, which expanded the opera's plotline and added extra characters, was dedicated to the Gnats. It reads like a cross between P.G. Wodehouse, Thorne Smith and *A Midsummer Night's Dream*.

Pamela Stigsby, daughter of an American dry-goods king, is infatuated with Charles, a young English lord (and vice versa), but her father refuses to countenance any son-in-law whose aristocratic pedigree does not run to a family ghost. The quick-thinking Charles claims that his ancestors were cursed with a family witch instead; he stages a mock seance and inadvertently conjures up Lady Angela, a real witch. A host of misunderstandings and misadventures ensue, particularly after Angela misplaces her wand. She finds herself smitten with Pamela's father and proposes to whisk him off to "witches land"; under her spell, two highly respectable dowagers are transformed into a monkey and a motorcar, the butler becomes a frog, and the local curate "comes to" taking a bath in the middle of a gravel drive! The butler subsequently becomes the unlikely object of adoration of most of the local female population. Naturally, everything resolves itself at the conclusion.[12]

ABC's considerable talent for characterization is well to the fore in *The Family Witch*, most notably in the set-piece scenes in which the socially competitive Mrs Parkinson-Trott and Miss Mewther fall victim to Angela's magic. Otherwise the novel, as a whole, remains mildly amusing but little more. The *Times Literary Supplement* acknowledged the "buoyant and unflagging manner" in which ABC recounted the story but implied that his writing skills were not well enough developed to render it really funny.[13] A second comic fantasy—an excursion into the realm of "biological science fiction" called *The Professor on Paws* (1926)—was somewhat more successful.

Professor Ridgeley, a distinguished scientist, believes it is possible to graft vital portions of brain tissue from a recently dead organism to a living one. He successfully produces a rabbit which can wag its tail like a fox terrier. When Ridgeley dies unexpectedly, his calculating colleague, Professor Cantrell, is bound by an agreement to undertake a final and convincing proof of the theory: he transfers part of Ridgeley's brain to the nearest available animal—a black kitten—with complete success.

Ridgeley is gratified at the vindication of his theory but much less so by the disadvantages of being a cat (particularly a lady cat, subject to the attentions of his daughter Marjorie's tomcat). He finds himself fussed and crooned over by elderly ladies and chased by dogs, has a tin can tied to his tail by street urchins, and endures being adopted by an actress, abducted and sold to an exhibitor of performing animals, and repossessed by the unscrupulous Cantrell. Ultimately, the professor is rescued by his daughter and her fiancé, and he and they acquire a fortune exhibiting his extraordinary powers in public. He enjoys great success spelling out letters and responding to general knowledge questions, but on the brink of an appearance tour of the United States, the effects of the experiment begin to wear off. The professor gradually reverts back to being just an ordinary black cat when Cantrell is unable to duplicate the operation. The novel concludes with Marjorie's discovery of four intelligent kittens (presumably her father's) in the spare bedroom.

The Professor on Paws was well received by the critics and was one of only two A.B. Cox books to be published in the United States. The *New York Times* dubbed it "a happy addition to the field of light fiction," and the *Times Literary Supplement* opined that "Mr. Cox's ingenuity in exploring all the amusing possibilities of the situation is most praise-worthy."[14]

In *The Wintringham Mystery*, a young woman disappears during a seance at a country house-party. Subsequent events indicate that her misadventure is part of an extortion attempt: the aristocrat hostess's jewelry goes missing and a furtive-looking butler is found dead. The puzzle is probed and ultimately solved by a gent "of reduced means" who, fortuitously, happens to be acting as the household's temporary footman. The story was serialized by the *Daily Mirror* in March-April 1926, with a 500-pound prize offered to any reader who could correctly deduce how, why and by whose agency, the victim (Stella) disappeared.

A first reading of *The Wintringham Mystery* suggests that it is a straightforward, if not very distinguished, detective story. However, a closer examination indicates that the whole thing is intended as a burlesque which satirizes (albeit with only limited success) the stock *dramatis personae* and situations of the modish puzzle story. The central abduction is real enough, but the apparent murder turns out to have been accidental, and the solution is an uninspired reworking of "the butler did it" (in collusion with the housemaid). The characters may well have owed something to Agatha Christie's *The Secret of Chimneys*, and are deliberately even more one-dimensional and predictable than usual. They include the requisite imperious dowager, a poisonous (and transparently Semitic) financier, a blustery Colonel, a bright young thing nicknamed Baby, a typical silly ass, a luckless flapper, an attractive young heiress who feels compelled by filial duty to affiance herself to the financier, and a penniless but personable young hero who loves her (and, of course, wins her at the conclusion).

The Wintringham Mystery is one of ABC's least effective efforts, and he undoubtedly recognized the fact. It was revised and republished (with a few name changes) in 1927, as *Cicely Disappears* by one A. Monmouth Platts. The pseudonym, only used this once, was drawn from the Iles family's traditional Watford address. The publisher was John Long, a specialist purveyor of lowbrow entertainment to the circulating libraries. Johns speculates on ABC's decision to release *Cicely Disappears* under the John Long imprimatur and a new pseudonym, and suggests that Collins may well have turned the book down as substandard. Possibly the terms of the *Daily Mirror* serialization precluded publication—hence ABC's ploy of posing as an unknown writer and altering the title and the protagonists' names.[15] Read today, *The Wintringham Mystery/Cicely Disappears* has little of the wit or flavor of the Anthony Berkeley books, although it should be noted that the amateur sleuth does come up with a plausible but incorrect solution to the puzzle—in the Roger Sheringham manner—before finally arriving at the truth.

Mr. Priestley's Problem (subtitled *An Extravaganza in Crime*) playfully sends up the standard penny-dreadful; it was published by Collins in 1927 (by Doubleday in the United States in 1928, as *The Amateur Crime*), and was an expansion of an unpublished short story called "Nothing Ever Happens."[16] Reprints of the book were issued under the Anthony Berkeley byline although (as Panek has noted) it is not really a detective story.[17] For one thing, there is no crime; the plot revolves around an elaborate practical joke. A group of amateur criminologists contrive a murder hoax. They are intent on studying at first hand the mind processes and reactions of a "killer." On the dubious premise that "he needs shaking up badly," Matthew Priestley, a shy and retiring little man ("as set and unenterprising as a man of sixty"), is selected to play the part of the unwitting guinea pig. Laura, an attractive flapper, accordingly enlists Priestley's aid in supposedly recovering some embarrassing correspondence; in the process, Priestley is led to believe that he has shot and killed the alleged blackmailer, and he finds himself on the run with the not uncongenial Laura. Chance conspires to have them bound together by handcuffs for a time.

Priestley finds himself unexpectedly enjoying the unfamiliar sensation of "living life with a capital L"; he has no regrets about apparently having rid the world of a ruthless blackmailer, and he finds himself strongly attracted to his young companion. Ultimately, he turns the tables on the plotters, gives them a taste of their own medicine (in a chaotic subplot involving the mythical Crown Prince of Bosnogovina), finds his life transformed in the process, and is united with a suitably subdued Laura at the fade-out.

Mr Priestley's Problem is a likeable romp, and an often clever burlesque of the thriller genre, although it tends to go on too long. (The retaliatory practical joke becomes rather tedious.) The development of the hero's relationship with his youthful fellow-fugitive is described very effectively, and the novel rejoices in a number of deliciously Wodehouse-style observations. For example, we are told that a disgruntled Laura "now wore the air of one who has stepped gaily on to a train labeled Birmingham, and finds herself in Crewe."[18] Charles Shibuk has judged the book one of ABC's best efforts of the 1920s, and suggests that the handcuffs sequence may well have inspired a similar motif in Alfred Hitchcock's film *The Thirty-Nine Steps*. (Handcuffs do not feature in John Buchan's original novel.)[19]

Priestley is the first of several meek, prissy yet unexpectedly resilient little men who feature throughout the Cox/Berkeley/Iles canon, and who may have had some resemblance to the author himself. (Others include Cyril Pinkerton, Mr Todhunter, Mr Chitterwick and—arguably—Dr Bickleigh.) ABC reproduced his exploits in a three-act stage play, variously titled *Mr Priestley's Adventure*, *Mr Priestley's Night Out*, *Mr Priestley's Problem* and *Handcuffs for Two*. The play was first produced at Brighton in March 1928 and subsequently moved on to London where it earned moderately favorable reviews. One critic, however, did take exception to the underlying cruelty of the practical joke perpetrated against the hero.[20]

Other Works by 'A.B. Cox'

ABC maintained his interest in music and the musical stage after his experience with the Gnats and *The Family Witch*. Symons remembers that he had a talent for writing "light, catchy tunes," a number of which he published at his own expense. Mostly waltzes, marches and ballads, and rejoicing in forgettable titles like "Dreaming of You" or "Five Little Petticoats," the songs had little lasting appeal, although several of them were performed publicly by Marion Milford, a professional singer and good friend of the composer.[21]

In 1928 the writer provided the book to J.J. Sterling Hill's music for *The Merchant Prince or The Pioneers of Aristocracy: A Comic Opera in the Gilbertian Tradition*. *The Merchant Prince* was a futuristic fantasy of village life, set 40 years in the future, when "commercial modes of thought have ousted all others," and the rural aristocracy has been displaced by a nouveau riche plutocracy. It was first staged at Watford by the local operatic society in May 1928, under the direction of composer Hill, and then moved to London's New Scala theatre for a short season. The *Times* reviewed the production kindly, called it "a remarkable achievement for amateurs," and noted that ABC's dialogue and lyrics were "fluent." However, the critic suggested that the two collaborators had so steeped themselves in the phraseology, gestures and conventions of the comic opera form that creative originality had been sacrificed in the process. (With that in mind, it seemed unlikely that the production would ever become a perennial with amateur societies.) A number of copies of the playscript of *The Merchant Prince* were bound and privately circulated. Johns describes one such in his bibliography, and another (ABC's own copy) was catalogued and sold by the Ulysses Bookshop in London in early 1994.[22]

Almost all ABC's published output under his own name was confined to the 1920s. The exceptions were the nonfiction *O England*, which I discuss in chapter 7, and two slim volumes of limericks. *A Pocketbook of 100 New Limericks* and *A Pocketbook of 100 More Limericks* were privately published by the author (as A.B. Cox Ltd, of 131a Eltham High Street, London) in 1959 and 1960 respectively. These booklets are among the rarest of ABC's titles (they are not listed in the catalogue of the British Library), but as Julian Symons has described their contents as "excruciatingly bad," this does not seem to be such a great loss. Symons remembers that the author distributed copies of the limited editions to friends and colleagues for Christmas. One of the items in the first collection is dedicated to Francis Iles, "a critic."[23]

Read today, the A.B. Cox sketches and comic novels are pleasant, undemanding, and—at their best—tinged with some of the wit and keen ironic observation that continue to make the author's crime fiction so enjoyable. In their own right though, they are generally of less interest than anything he wrote under his Berkeley or Iles guises. The novels have little of the timeless appeal of Wodehouse, for instance (ABC was an ardent fan of that master humorist, and dedicated *Trial and Error* to him),[24] while the sketches are inconsequential in the main, and now notable primarily because they represent a great crime-writer's literary apprenticeship. As a stereotyped product of the 1920s (dare I say a more innocent age), they suffer from their lack of sophistication, but they do shed some light on their historico-social context. Ayresome Johns has written of the *Down Our Road series:* "Although these sketches are perhaps individually of little value, it is possible to trace the development of Cox's skill at depicting the environment of such classics as *Malice Aforethought*. And where, if not here, did he tune his often marvellous ear for dialogue?"[25] I look next at the flowering of A.B. Cox's promise in the Berkeley and Iles novels and short stories.

4

ANTHONY BERKELEY (I):
ROGER SHERINGHAM

In an early contribution to *Punch,* ABC noted that he had always nurtured a mild ambition to write a detective story: "There must be something very fascinating in fitting the history of a diabolical and seemingly insoluble crime into a neat, compact little pattern, with the ingenious explanation in the last sentence or two." Intimating that he had recently started work on just such a project, he offered readers the prototype for future "arresting" opening paragraphs: "Colonel Grant flung the stub-end of his cigar through the open window before which he was standing, shrugged his shoulders and made a half-turn towards the room behind him. Before he could complete the movement his knees crumpled up beneath him, and he fell dead."

Who or what killed Colonel Grant, why and how, we will never know. One possibility mooted by ABC was that the colonel may have been overcome by "a poisoned thorn exhaled from a native blowpipe"[1] (A similar means of annihilation is used in the author's penultimate novel, *Death in the House.)*

This tongue-in-cheek little sketch was the earliest indication of ABC's keenness to try his hand at detective fiction. He subsequently parodied the standard detective, mystery and suspense tales in a series of humorous essays for *Punch,* reprinted in *Jugged Journalism.* Among his comic examples were "Holmes and the Dasher," a delicious Sherlock Holmes spoof written in the style of P.G. Wodehouse, and "Bitter Almonds," in which an amorous young man accosts a particularly unresponsive girl on a train—he discovers she is dead from cyanide poisoning. These short burlesques, while amusing, are inconsequential as detection, but they hint at ABC's affinity with the genre, and anticipate the direction his career was to take. In one sketch he summarized the formula:

First of all think of a murder (a sound jewel robbery, with plenty of titled names in it, will do at a pinch; but there's nothing like a good, juicy murder); then formulate a set of circumstances under which it could not possibly have been committed; surround the victim with several persons all of whom had an excellent motive for murdering him, but none of whom could possibly have done so; and go ahead.[2]

By simply juggling the time-honored ingredients of omniscient detective, obtuse policeman, timetables and so on, ABC suggested (perhaps rather ingenuously) that the merest hack writer was able to concoct a successful detective story. "Having begun with a facile indication of how easy it would be to create a popular success from mediocre materials," writes William Bradley Strickland, "[ABC] took the next logical step," and he realized his ambition in the stories and books he published under the pseudonym Anthony Berkeley.[3]

ABC's first use of the Berkeley byline was for a comic sketch, "Telling The Tale," and a dozen or so similar pieces for *The Humorist* in 1923-24. They are indistinguishable from the material ABC was publishing as A.B. Cox at the time, and it seems likely that the pen name was employed merely so he could submit more than one sketch at a time to the magazine.[4] Once he was well and truly launched as a detective writer, however, ABC formally adopted the Berkeley pseudonym and persona to distinguish his crime fiction from his comic writing.

"Anthony Berkeley" achieved fame and substantial popularity in his day, as the creator of Roger Sheringham, one of the Golden Age's more colorful and distinctive amateur sleuths. Sheringham was a diverting and refreshing alternative to the investigators who dominated crime fiction at the time. By making his hero bluff, prone to error and recognizably human, ABC/Berkeley, in the words of Howard Haycraft, brought to the detective novel "an urbane and naturalistic quality that was a welcome and needed relief."[5] ABC/Berkeley failed to see why "even a detective story should not aim at the creation of a natural atmosphere, just as much as any other work of the lighter fiction". Accordingly, his sleuth was "far removed from a sphinx" and not above making "a mistake or two occasionally."[6]

Overbearing, loquacious, vain, sometimes astonishingly self-confident, Roger Sheringham was once described by his creator as "an offensive person, founded on an offensive person I once knew, because in my original innocence I thought it would be amusing to have an offensive detective."[7] As such, Sheringham was first intended as a satirical figure, conceived as the very antithesis of the "Great Detective."[8] Strickland has observed: "Sheringham appears as a loud meddler, painted broadly as a beer-drinking, abrasive, self-centered, rude man, at once absurdly vain and cynically deprecatory of public taste and intelligence; and, above all, bull-headed to a fault."[9] According to Leroy Panek: "[Berkeley], I think, asked himself what kind of man would have the gall to push himself into other people's private affairs, to intrude where he is not wanted, to assume the duties of others, the police, and to have sublime faith in his own perception and acumen. His answer was a very disagreeable one."[10]

Given the popularity of the novels, and the fact that readers apparently took the character quite seriously, ABC/Berkeley subsequently felt the need to tone down Sheringham. ("Roger-the-detective was anxious not to resemble the usual pompous and irritating detective of fiction. . . . As a result he went perhaps too far to the other extreme and erred on the side of breeziness.")[11] In time Sheringham took on some of the more conservative characteristics of his fictional peers, and in one book, *Panic Party*, found himself obliged to play the traditional thriller hero. Yet, throughout his incarnations, the sleuth retained an unfailing confidence in his own deductive ability (notwithstanding a number of spectacular failures and near-misses), a radical and individualistic conception of justice (he assisted more than one apparent murderer to escape retribution because of his belief that the victim was of much more value dead than alive), and an ultimately engaging *joie de vivre*.

The Cases

Sheringham appeared in ten full-length novels and five short stories, published between 1925 and 1943; a sixth short story (in two versions), a stage play (based on one of the novels) and a radio play were belatedly published in 1994. As well, the character was one of the four amateur sleuths brought in to solve the murder of a newspaper tycoon in the Detection Club's collaborative effort *Ask a Policeman* (1933). In that instance, Sheringham's exploits were recorded—and parodied—by Dorothy L. Sayers. (ABC performed the same service with Lord Peter Wimsey.) Sheringham was also one of a number of popular fictional sleuths whose mannerisms and stylistic idiosyncrasies were emulated by Agatha Christie's Tommy and Tuppence in *Partners in Crime* (1929).

Readers first encountered Sheringham in *The Layton Court Mystery*, which ABC published anonymously in 1925.[12] The plot finds Sheringham and his close friend, Alec Grierson, guests at a country house-party hosted by Victor Stanworth, a genial collector of celebrities. When Stanworth is found shot dead in his library, Roger gleefully seizes the chance to play detective, and he enlists a skeptical Alec as his Watson. It soon becomes clear that the seemingly benign victim had been a thoroughly unsavory blackmailer, and that everyone at Layton Court has a motive for his murder. After numerous false starts, Sheringham finally elaborates a plausible solution; he is more than a little irritated when his theory, which implicates Stanworth's ex-army officer secretary, proves to be incorrect. ("He didn't kill Stanworth at all. It's extremely annoying of him considering how neatly I solved this little problem of ours.")

ABC dedicated *The Layton Court Mystery* to his father (also a mystery enthusiast), and later noted that he wrote the book for "the sheer fun of it," just to see whether he could.[13] Sheringham's first case is a bright and breezy effort, which remains amusing and readable today. While more than one writer has hailed ABC/Berkeley's supremely self-confident amateur sleuth as the successor to E.C. Bentley's similarly fallible Philip Trent, it is interesting that no one has pointed out that Sheringham does finally uncover the truth of the Layton Court puzzle or, indeed, that the solution actually anticipates (at least in part) Agatha Christie and *The Murder of Roger Ackroyd!*

The popularity of his first foray into the genre persuaded ABC the experiment was worth repeating. The fact that detective stories paid rather better than the humorous sketches he was contributing to *Punch, London Opinion* and other periodicals, certainly influenced his decision. (He once remarked: "When I find something that pays better than detective stories I shall write that.")[14] For the second Roger Sheringham book, he drew on his extensive knowledge of real-life criminology.

Florence Maybrick was found guilty of administering a fatal dose of arsenic to her husband in 1889, and sentenced to hang. (The sentence was later commuted.) Ever since, generations of amateur and professional criminologists have debated whether she or someone else was responsible, whether James Maybrick committed suicide, or whether, in fact, the poisoning might have been accidental. J.S. Fletcher, for one, has concluded that Maybrick's propensity for arsenic-eating (as a restorative) predisposed him to gastroenteritis, and thus he probably died of natural causes.[15] ABC subscribed to the same theory and reprised the Maybrick scenario and *dramatis personae* (hypochondriac victim, adulterous young wife, her lover, vengeful brother-in-law, spiteful parlormaid) as the Bentley murder in *The Wychford Poisoning Case* (1926).

When Mrs Bentley is charged with killing her husband, the case attracts a blaze of publicity. There seems to be little doubt of her guilt. Sheringham, however, is dissatisfied: the evidence seems almost too damning. Remarking that "it'd be nice to unearth the truth and prove everybody else in the whole blessed country wrong," he enlists the aid of Alec Grierson again, and they hasten down to Wychford, the scene of the crime. Conveniently, Alec has relatives living at Wychford, and his young cousin (a stereotyped 1920s flapper named Sheila) joins the sleuths in their quest for an answer to the puzzle.

ABC notes in the book's preface that *The Wychford Poisoning Case* is an attempt "to substitute for the materialism of the usual crime-puzzle of fiction those psychological values which are . . . the basis of the universal interest in the far more absorbing criminological dramas of real life." "It's the human element that makes the crime possible," declares Roger, "and it's the human element which ought to lead us to the truth."[16] His fascination with the psychology of the Bentley household seduces him into concluding that the unbalanced victim (Bentley) had suicided in such a way that suspicion would fall on his wife and she would be hanged for murder. As at Layton Court, Sheringham discovers that his carefully elaborated solution is wrong, that he has "paid too much attention to the psychological possibilities and not enough to hard fact." (He does have the satisfaction of ultimately ensuring that the charges against Mrs Bentley are dropped.)

Charles Shibuk calls *The Wychford Poisoning Case* ABC/Berkeley's weakest effort, and the author himself once declared it "fit only for incineration."[17] Certainly, it is not without flaws. Dashiell Hammett dubbed the conclusion "flabby" and "unsporting" (although that is a matter of opinion), and 1990s sensibility might rightly object to the attitudes to women expressed by both Roger and his "Watson."[18] (I know one female Berkeley enthusiast who had difficulty restraining herself from throwing the book across the room because of Alec's treatment of Sheila.) Nor, as Panek has pointed out, does Berkeley achieve his aim of giving the reader a "psychological" novel.[19] (He would do so a few years later, of course, with *Trial and Error* and the Francis Iles books.) Still, the novel is never less than entertaining, it sparkles with humor, and it contains a good deal of diverting comment on famous crimes and criminals. It also provides us with a more complete picture of Sheringham than any of the other books (and before his creator started to tone him down). Interestingly, Barzun and Taylor, who have distinct reservations about almost all the Berkeley books, make an exception of *The Wychford Poisoning Case,* observing that "the study of arsenical poisoning, the asides on the law, and the doctrine on love, boredom and adultery are all good."[20]

The Vane Mystery (first published as *Roger Sheringham and the Vane Mystery* in 1927, and in the United States as *The Mystery at Lover's Cave*), is the first of eight occasions in which Sheringham matches wits, or collaborates, with Chief Inspector Moresby of Scotland Yard.[21] By this stage, Roger is entrenched as regular crime columnist for the *Daily Courier* newspaper. When a woman falls to her death from a Hampshire cliff-top, his editor scents a possible news story and sends special correspondent Sheringham off to Ludmouth to investigate. He takes along his young cousin, Anthony Walton, who promptly falls head-over-heels in love with the police's chief suspect. (Chief Inspector Moresby's presence on the scene confirms that Mrs Vane's death involved foul play.) The situation is complicated by a second murder: the dead woman's disreputable first husband is at Ludmouth, disguised as a clergyman. He is killed when the poison aconitine is placed in his pipe.

Roger bows to no one in his estimate of his own "astuteness and cunning"; he is convinced he can solve the case before Moresby can, and he looks forward to triumphing over official-dom. After dismissing the real culprit as psychologically inca-pable of murder, Sheringham constructs an ingenious hypothesis: Mrs Vane, who was being blackmailed by Meadows, her first hus-band, placed poison in his pipe tobacco. He subsequently pushed her over the cliff. "Result, Meadows murdered Mrs Vane and Mrs Vane murdered Meadows, in spite of the handicap of being already dead herself." ("I should think that must be the first time in Scotland Yard's history that a man has been murdered by a corpse," muses Roger.)[22] Moresby's complete rejection of his theory represents the nadir of Sheringham's detecting career. The Chief Inspector proves that the case is as straightforward as any he has ever come across. He chides Roger for allowing his over-abundant imagination to introduce "all sorts of irrelevant issues" into what was just "a simple little murder."

The normally ebullient Roger leaves Ludmouth thoroughly humiliated, but he is able to turn the tables on Moresby in *The Silk Stocking Murders* (1928) nine months later. In his capacity as "criminological expert and purveyor of chattily-written articles on murder" for the *Daily Courier*, Sheringham receives a letter from a rural vicar pleading for help in tracing his daughter. Janet Man-ners has gone up to London to find work as an actress and then disappeared; she turns out to be one of a spate of apparent sui-cides—young women found hanged by their own silk stockings. Roger concludes that a serial killer is at work, and he promptly undertakes inquiries, assisted by the fiancés of two of the mur-dered women, and the vicar's personable younger daughter, Anne. He flushes out the murderer by using Anne in a harrowing reconstruction of the crimes.

The Silk Stocking Murders is rather more serious than its prede-cessors. There is nothing remotely "acceptable" about the crimes: none of the victims can be said to deserve their fate, the killer is revealed as an extremely dangerous madman, and this is the only novel in which Sheringham gladly hands the culprit over to the law. Both Shibuk and Strickland praise the book (Shibuk argues that its seriousness represents an advance in ABC/Berkeley's work) but, in my view, the zest and humor which make the first three books so enjoyable are sacrificed here somewhat to the sensational nature of the murders and the startling climax.[23] I tend to agree with the contemporary reviewer who wrote: "*The Silk Stocking Murders* has few claims to distinction . . . it would pass well enough as a run-of-the-mine detective story; in the limelight it reveals too many flaws."[24] With Roger more subdued than usual, the book is even a little dull in parts; it is also marred by a number of gratuitous anti-Semitic references (these do provide us with an insight into 1920s social attitudes).[25] It is not without its charms however, most notably the mutually productive unofficial partnership which forms between Sheringham and Moresby in the course of the investigation. The Chief Inspector, who after Ludmouth had dismissed Roger as "a volatile-witted amateur intent only upon proving impossible theories of his own erection," now develops an appreciation of his erstwhile colleague's "quick grasp of essentials" and of the value of his "vivid imagination" when brought to bear on a problem. For his part, Sheringham is unexpectedly impressed by Moresby's common sense and encompassing knowledge of criminal history. Respect does not stop him from gloating when he triumphs over the police at the end of the novel.[26]

The next Sheringham case, his investigation of the poisoned chocolates murder, is justifiably regarded as the Berkeley masterpiece. Its first manifestation was as "The Avenging Chance" (1929), which Ellery Queen has called "as nearly a perfectly plotted short story as has been written." (Queen included it among his 'Golden dozen' of "all time detective story gems.")[27] A box of chocolates is mailed to the crusty Sir William Anstruther at his club. Anstruther loathes chocolates and so readily gives them to another club member, Graham Beresford, who wants them so he can square a wager with his wife. Beresford becomes ill and his wife dies after tasting the chocolates (which have been injected with nitrobenzine). With the police completely baffled by the case, Moresby is keen to see what Sheringham can make of it. Roger believes that Chance "the avenger" will step in and provide the clue needed to solve the puzzle, and by sheer luck, he obtains a vital link which indicates that Mrs Beresford had *not* been killed by mistake.

"The Avenging Chance" offered readers one answer to the question, Who murdered Joan Beresford? Roger's deductions and conclusions were reprised when the story was expanded into *The Poisoned Chocolates Case* (1929). This time round though, his is only one of six solutions! ABC/Berkeley recapitulates the crime circumstances and protagonists (with a few name changes: the Beresfords become Mr and Mrs Bendix, Sir William Anstruther becomes Sir Eustace Pennefather), but in the novel Moresby presents the problem to the combined ingenuity of the prestigious Crime Circle.

The Crime Circle (a fictional version of the Detection Club which ABC was instrumental in founding in 1928) is an exclusive organization founded and presided over by Sheringham, and limited to six members with particular talent for "criminological investigation": a famous lawyer, a popular lady-dramatist, a noted novelist (possibly a caricature of Dorothy L. Sayers), a detective-story-writer, Roger and the seemingly ineffectual Mr Ambrose Chitterwick. Each member applies his/her wits, experience or intuition to the puzzle, and comes up with a hypothesis. Not surprisingly, it is the inexperienced little Mr Chitterwick who finally plumbs the truth of the mystery.

Julian Symons calls *The Poisoned Chocolates Case* "one of the most stunning trick stories in the history of detective fiction."[28] Its multiple deductions and audacious denouement are an unrivaled tour de force, and the author's satirical characterizations (particularly the Crime Circle members) continue to delight modern readers. The parallels between each of the six theories (seven, if we include the police view that a disinterested criminal lunatic is responsible) and famous true murder cases (Marie LaFarge, Molineux, Christina Edmunds, etc.) remain a particularly noteworthy feature of the novel. It earned deservedly good reviews on its release, and it is the only Berkeley title still reprinted regularly. Christianna Brand suggested yet another possible outcome of the plot in a 1979 edition.[29]

The Second Shot (1930) is also an expansion of a short story. In "Perfect Alibi," an unprincipled but good-looking bounder, Eric Scott-Davies, is shot dead at a country house-party.[30] The police conclude that the death was accidental, but the Chief Constable remains mildly unconvinced. The other members of the house-party include Scott-Davies's young cousin (and heir), his fiancée, a married woman with whom he is having an affair, her long-suffering husband, and Cyril Pinkerton, a writer (a "prim, precise, conceited little ass with pince-nez and a dashed superior smile"). Virtually every one of them has a motive for Scott-Davies's death—not least Pinkerton, who had been publicly humiliated by him. Sheringham offers an armchair solution: Scott-Davies had betrayed a village maiden, and her father, the local policeman, then avenged the family honor.

ABC/Berkeley retained the short story's conclusion in the novel, but as the solution to a game of "Murder" played by the guests, and devised by the host (a mystery-writer). Scott-Davies is killed in reality while playing the part of the victim in the game. Pinkerton, who narrates the novel, becomes the chief suspect, and he calls in Sheringham, an old school-fellow. Sheringham proves that virtually anyone could have been the culprit, then diverts the police into accepting a theory of "ordinary, prosaic accident." If ever a man deserved shooting, it was Scott-Davies (assesses Roger), and he is quite prepared to fake evidence and perjure himself to ensure the guilty person (in Sheringham's view, the victim's fiancée) is not suspected. As is so often the case, Roger's deductions are flawed—it is Pinkerton who subtly triumphs at the end. (He gets the girl and provides the answer to the puzzle. He has been guilty all along!)

In the foreword to *The Second Shot,* Berkeley discusses the need for the detective novel to evolve from the pure puzzle to the study of criminal personality. The character of Pinkerton acts as a bridge between the Roger Sheringham whodunits (and whodunit burlesques) and the Francis Iles novels. Panek calls *The Second Shot* a "failed attempt" to overcome the genre's limitations, but Pinkerton's humorous narration gives the book an added dimension.[31] It remains an effective, if not outstanding, production, of which the *Times Literary Supplement* noted: "The slipshod reader will be puzzled at various stages of the narrative, but the careful one will agree that Mr Berkeley's experiment has proved most successful, and that he has played fair."[32]

Moresby and Sheringham team up to investigate the strangling (with a rosary) of an elderly woman in a shabby block of flats in *Top Storey Murder* (1931). Moresby believes the crime must be the work of one of a small number of professional burglars; Sheringham thinks the culprit is more likely to be a relative or neighbor of the dead woman. (The inhabitants of Monmouth Mansions are described as "persons with claims, genuine or imagined, to gentility, but little beyond the absence . . . of a Cockney accent to support them.") In the course of the inquiry, he finds himself strongly attracted to the victim's niece—partly because she is persistently unimpressed with him—and he impulsively engages her as his secretary. Much of the book's humor derives from their confrontations. *Top Storey Murder* gives us one of Roger's more spectacular blunders when he develops a watertight theory which casts the girl as the killer. He just manages to pass his mistake off as a joke after Moresby informs him that the real culprit has been apprehended. Reviews of the book (which was published as *Top Story Murder* in the United States) were rather lukewarm although critic James Sandoe once judged it the best of the Berkeley novels.[33]

Shibuk calls *Murder in the Basement* (1932) a "prime example of the British fair-play school and a straightforward, solid tale that is unjustly forgotten today."[34] Its premise and execution are more serious than most of the Sheringham cases, but (for me) the book works better than *The Silk Stocking Murders*, say, perhaps because most of the focus is on Moresby. The school setting and its dynamics are particularly well drawn, and invite comparison with Hugh Walpole's tortured common-room in *Mr Perrin and Mr Traill*. ("I never saw so many undercurrents among a small body of people in my life," maintains Roger.)

Moresby is called in when a couple of newlyweds discover a woman's body in the basement of their suburban house. Painstaking police work finally identifies the victim as a secretary at a rural prep school. As luck would have it, Sheringham has recently spent a fortnight at the school ("more for a joke than anything else"); intrigued by the internal conflict there, he has started a novel using the staff as characters. He loans the manuscript to Moresby, thus giving the policeman (and the reader) the chance to guess the identity and motive of the murderer. On this occasion, Moresby is (understandably) misled; Sheringham pinpoints the real killer but wisely allows the police conclusion to stand.

Barzun and Taylor call *Jumping Jenny* (1933; published in the United States as *Dead Mrs Stratton*) "beyond doubt, the poorest Berkeley extant," but they would seem to represent a definite minority view.[35] *Jumping Jenny* is a wonderfully frivolous and tricky exercise, which the *Times Literary Supplement* dubbed "one of the cleverest and most provoking detective stories that we have read for a long time."[36] Sheringham attends a "murder-victim" party given by a famous detective writer, at which all the guests impersonate famous killers. (Roger goes as George Joseph Smith of the "Brides in the Bath" fame.) Part of the party's macabre decor is a mock gallows from which three dummies are suspended. Among the other guests is the neurotic Ena Stratton, an obnoxious and embarrassingly unpleasant woman about whom someone remarks: "Something ought to be done about her. She's a danger to the community." Not surprisingly, Mrs. Stratton replaces one of the dummies on the gallows before the night is over.

Jumping Jenny plays fast and loose with the whodunit tradition: we see the murder committed, and know the murderer's identity (or think we do).[37] From then on, we watch the efforts of Sheringham and the other party guests as they strive to ensure that a verdict of suicide is brought in at the inquest. Ena Stratton's death is universally regarded as a blessing, and Roger wastes no sentiment on duty to the police. Admittedly, he is rather disconcerted when he is suspected of being the killer. (One of those present speculates: "You're the most officious person I know, and the most self-confident. If anyone in the world could commit an entirely spiritual, altruistic, infernally officious murder, it's you.") However, ABC/Berkeley has one last surprise in store. At the very end of the novel, he confounds the reader with a totally unexpected final twist (one of which Sheringham never becomes aware).

Milward Kennedy, a rather more orthodox Golden Age practitioner than his compatriot, once challenged ABC to write a novel in which the only interest would be the detection. Not only was ABC loath to do anything "so tedious," but (as he noted in the book's dedication to Kennedy) he designed *Panic Party* (1934) to do precisely the opposite. In the book (which was published in the United States as *Mr Pidgeon's Island*), Sheringham is invited to join 13 other guests on a luxury cruise presided over by Guy Pidgeon, a wealthy former Oxford don. Pidgeon has deliberately selected a heterogeneous mix of people so he can observe their interactions; they include a couple of aristocrats, a nouveau riche industrialist and his wife, an African explorer, a popular novelist and a gossip columnist. The party disembarks on an uncharted island only to find it is stranded there for at least a fortnight. The situation becomes sinister when Pidgeon (inspired by J.M. Barrie's *Shall We Join the Ladies*) tells his guests that there is a murderer amongst them, and that he plans to expose him/her once they all return to civilization. Although he confesses to Roger that he has concocted the whole scenario for his own entertainment, Pidgeon is killed during the night. From that point until the yacht returns, Roger tries simultaneously to solve the murder and to keep a lid on the hysteria mounting around him.

Panic Party is something of a hybrid. It has a number of the standard trappings of the traditional whodunit, such as a map of the island and a diagram of the camp; Roger actively searches for clues, interviews suspects and even takes fingerprints (although he does not recognize his own!). The book also becomes a thriller, as we watch the deterioration of morale and the veneer of civilization on the island. As Sheringham observes: "Under acute stress civilized people evidently revert to the primitive a great deal more quickly than one would ever have imagined." He becomes something of a heroic figure as he deals with a series of crises, and is knocked out, shot at and tied up in the process. Only the unexpected reappearance of the yacht averts disaster at the climax. (Roger solves the murder and later confronts the killer in London, but he chooses to do nothing more about it.)

The book has been rather underrated. While the mix of detection and adventure is somewhat uneasy, *Panic Party* is nevertheless a thought-provoking and skillful study of people under extreme pressure, and quite unlike any of the other Sheringham cases. The isolated setting invites comparison with Agatha Christie's *And Then There Were None* of course, but plot developments like the transformation of a sensible, no-nonsense career-woman into a hysterical virago echo the author's Francis Iles persona. The general absence of Roger's customary humor suggests that ABC felt he had well-nigh exhausted his detective-hero's possibilities by this time.

Panic Party was the last Sheringham book, but ABC/Berkeley featured him in another four short stories. In "White Butterfly" (1936), Moresby suggests he apply "psychology" to tracing the disappearance of a small-town solicitor's wife.[38] The solicitor maintains she has run off with her married lover, but local gossip suggests that he has murdered her. ABC had a poor opinion of the story which finds Roger in vintage erratic form; he correctly pinpoints the woman's burial place but targets the wrong suspect. He believes the husband is responsible. Fortunately, the police misunderstand his musings, and thanks to a vital clue (a mutilated butterfly), Roger is able to identify the killer. He has no hesitation in taking full credit for the solution.

In "The Wrong Jar" (1940), he investigates a village poisoning, in which the victim's husband is again the chief suspect. The plot, which involves access to a doctor's dispensary, and the dispatching of a love-rival, is a variant on the story line of the novel *Not to Be Taken* (which does not feature Sheringham).[39] For once, Roger acts as nemesis; rather in the style of Lord Peter Wimsey, he allows the unsympathetic culprit the option of suicide provided she writes a confession letter to the police.

The final Sheringham investigation published in the author's lifetime was "Mr Bearstowe Says" (1943), which is a mature version of a short story called "Razor-Edge" and a two-part radio play called "Red Anemones" (broadcast by the BBC in June 1940).[40] A chance remark heard at a Bloomsbury party leads Roger to the truth behind a suspicious drowning two years later. Puzzled by discrepancies in a missing persons report, he uses the clues of a razor and shaving soap to uncover an impersonation and identify a murderer. "Razor-Edge" and "Red Anemones" were published for the first time, together with "Mr. Bearstowe Says," in the 1994 compilation *The Roger Sheringham Stories.*

The typescript of another short story (in two versions) was found among ABC's papers, and both variants ("Double Bluff" and "Direct Evidence") were published in 1994. Presumably written in the 1920s, the story (or stories) team Sheringham with Alec Grierson once more. The duo is called on to investigate the drive-by shooting of a married femme fatale. Several witnesses testify to having seen her lover commit the crime, yet the hapless young man insists he was 10 miles away at the time. The two variants of the story strongly resemble each other; "Double Bluff" appears to be the revised version. (It contains extra characters and a completely different culprit and motive.)[41]

The Roger Sheringham Stories includes the script of a three-act play *Temporary Insanity*, based on *The Layton Court Mystery*, plus a *very* minor spoof titled "The Body's Upstairs," signed by A.B. Cox, "with apologies to Anthony Berkeley." Johns believes that the play was written as a follow-up to the stage version of *Mr Priestley's Problem* but was apparently never produced. (It is generally faithful to the novel.) In "The Body's Upstairs," Roger is called upon to locate a brilliant idea for the Christmas number of *London Opinion*. The sketch was obviously produced for that magazine (circa 1926), but it does not seem to have been published at that time.[42]

Johns notes that three fragments of projected Sheringham novels also exist. Two of the fragments detail breakfast conversations, one between Roger and Alec Grierson (about gas poisonings) and the other between Sheringham and his nephew. A more extensive draft exists of the beginning of another novel, which deals with the mysterious disappearance and reappearance of a corpse. The manuscript indicates that Roger was to be called in to investigate the mystery.[43]

No listing of the Sheringham cases would be complete without at least a mention of *Ask a Policeman* (1933), a collaborative novel by the Detection Club in which the contributors swapped their trademark investigators. ABC/Berkeley chronicled Lord Peter Wimsey's efforts to track down the killer of a press baron (see chapter 5 for detail) while Dorothy L. Sayers rendered an affectionate parody of Sheringham. In "The Conclusions of Mr Roger Sheringham" our hero is depicted as vibrantly energetic, given to darting all over the place, and not averse to impersonating a suspect in order to obtain evidence. He identifies the dead man's chauffeur as the culprit. Moresby praises his solution as "extremely ingenious," but "as regards its being the truth—?"

In the course of his detecting career, lasting from 1925 to 1943, Roger Sheringham investigates strangulations, poisonings, shootings, two cases where the victim is pushed off a cliff, and one forcible drowning. Death proves to be natural in one case and accidental in another. Sheringham solves the mystery in only half the books (although his success rate is considerably higher in the short stories—perhaps because their length did not allow ABC the space for Roger to develop elaborate incorrect theories and still arrive at the truth). In only two of the novels is the killer apprehended by the law. Much of the appeal of the Sheringham cases undoubtedly lies in this nonconformity, and in the sleuth's idiosyncratic personality and attitudes, including his individualistic conception of law versus natural justice (probably a reflection of the author's own views). For detail, we need to look more closely at Sheringham himself.

The Character

ABC/Berkeley provided readers with a short biography of his detective-hero, "Concerning Roger Sheringham" as the foreword to *Dead Mrs Stratton* (the United States edition of *Jumping Jenny*), and we can glean further details of Roger's appearance, personality, history, attitudes and idiosyncrasies from the books and stories. Although author and character were poles apart physically and temperamentally, ABC used Sheringham as a vehicle for expressing his own opinions on literature, law and British society, and he endowed the sleuth with many features of his own middle-class background.

Roger Sheringham was born in 1891, the only son of a doctor in a provincial town near London (possibly Watford?). We can deduce that he had at least one sister as a fragment from an unpublished novel describes him having breakfast with a nephew, Maurice.[44] As was customary for the sons of professional men, he was first educated at the local day school, then as a boarder at Roland House in Surrey (which features in *Murder in the Basement*). At age 14, he won a scholarship to an ancient public school—one of those institutions "which despise Eton and Harrow just as thoroughly as Eton and Harrow ignore them." (In *The Layton Court Mystery* the school is said to be Winchester; elsewhere we are told it was Fernhurst.) It was there that Roger became acquainted with Cyril Pinkerton, who was to enlist his aid years later in *The Second Shot*. Pinkerton remembered him as "a very ordinary—and indeed somewhat offensive!—small boy." According to Dorothy L. Sayers (who parodied the sleuth in *Ask a Policeman*), another schoolmate was Hilary Muggleton-Blood, future chaplain to the Archbishop of the Midlands, who recalled that the young Sheringham was popularly known as "Snotty."

Roger went up to Oxford in 1910, either to Merton College or the fictional St Mary's. (He first met the classics don, Guy Pidgeon of *Panic Party*, at the latter.) He played rugby for his college, reportedly excelled at diving, won a Blue for golf in his last year, and took out a second-class degree in classics and history just before the Great War shut down Oxford. Like his creator, Sheringham was wounded while serving in France; he was twice recommended for the Military Cross and once for the Distinguished Service Order, and we are told he was privately "very annoyed" not to be awarded either. After the war, he spent "spasmodic interludes" in business, as a schoolmaster, and as a chicken farmer. He also tried his hand at writing and had the good fortune to dash off a best-selling novel. Thereafter, he became financially independent through his writing, which eventually included a regular column for the *Daily Courier*. (One of his novels, *Pamela Alive*, went into seven editions in five weeks!)

By the time of his visit to Layton Court, Sheringham has become sufficiently well-to-do to be able to indulge his pet hobby of criminology at leisure. His public school and university background enable him to move in (relatively) exalted circles: he is acquainted with Lord Peter Wimsey, for instance, and he has sufficient influence to extract an extra special license from a bishop (thus ensuring that Pinkerton and Armorel Scott-Davies marry before they are called upon to testify against each other in *The Second Shot*).[45] Sheringham has rooms at the prestigious Albany where he is valeted by a Bunter-like domestic (Bunter is Wimsey's man-servant) named Meadows. Meadows is a model servant who waxes reproachful only on the rare occasions his employer is late for lunch. Roger displays a keen appreciation for good food, particularly Tripes a la mode de Caen (with which he is known to tempt the Chief Inspector), and he is devoted to quality beer (such as Berkshire 5X). He is also an enthusiastic bridge-player. In *The Poisoned Chocolates Case* he is described as a gentleman "pretending not to be"—in contrast to the detective novelist, Harrogate Bradley, who desperately wants to be seen as a gentleman, and envies Roger accordingly.

In appearance, Sheringham is described as "a stockily-built man" of between 30 and 40, somewhat below average height, with a round rather long face, "two shrewd, twinkling grey eyes," and a "rather wide mouth." His clothes, which typically run to "perfectly shapeless grey flannel trousers," a disreputable old Norfolk jacket (its pockets bulging with papers), and "an inconceivably shapeless hat," seem to "argue a certain eccentricity and contempt for convention that is just a little too self-conscious to be quite natural, without going so far as to degenerate into a pose." He is cheerfully addicted to "poisoning the fragrant atmosphere with clouds of evil smoke" from a "particularly unsavoury" short-stemmed pipe.[46]

Sheringham's whole approach to life and crime is informed by his reserves of unbounded, exuberant energy. According to his creator, he is "one of those dynamic persons who seem somehow to live two minutes to everybody else's one." Single-minded, with room for only one enthusiasm at a time, be it applied psychopathy, murder, literature or beer, he will constitute himself an authority on any subject at the drop of a hat. His volubility is described as "nothing short of amazing" (hardly anyone else can get a word in), and the "spontaneous heartiness" of his voice has been known to grate intolerably on his listeners. The opening scene of *The Wychford Poisoning Case* finds him expounding "oracularly" on the likeness of life to kedgeree—both are potentially either delightful or "utterly mournful."

Although he displays a keen intellectual interest in modern literature (he thoroughly enjoys a discussion on Masefield in *Top Storey Murder*, for example), Sheringham has little time for the pretensions of Bloomsbury, and is rather disdainful of 1920s culture. He maintains that the "modern girl" needs spanking, and he sneers at the trendy "frog-faced" young men and their Amazon partners who frequent fashionable Soho night-spots. In an amusing dig at ABC's literary apprenticeship, Sheringham reads *Punch* from cover to cover "to induce sleep," and dismisses the readers of *London Opinion* as middle class. He is uncharacteristically self-deprecating about his own writing. While he realizes that being Roger Sheringham, the celebrated novelist, enables him to worm his way into people's good graces (an advantage when detecting), and allows him to breakfast unceremoniously in his dressing-gown ("the sole remnant of a robust bohemianism"), he has no illusions about the quality of his output. Unlike most novelists, opines ABC/Berkeley, Roger is a realist in this regard, and he concurs when Alec calls his writing "tripe." Abuse of his work actually fills our hero with "combative joy," as when an American reviewer lambastes the "ponderous attempts at humour" in his latest opus. ("There is no taking the *Chicago News* for a joy-ride," he gleefully admits.) Popular novelist Angela St Thomas dubs his crime articles "potboilers," but she concedes that they contain a lot of sense. ("I was trying to write down to the standard of the ordinary *Courier* reader," is his claim.) To Mrs Purefoy, a genuine admirer of his books, Roger says: "I hope you enjoyed reading them more than I did the writing of them." Rather than being happy only with a pen in his hand, he insists that, like most writers, he is only happy when the pen is out of his hand. ABC confides that this is something of a pose on Sheringham's part, that he must write or explode; when he argues that only second-rate writers take themselves or their work too seriously, his compensatory "I write for a living" is, of course, no less of a pose. In *Murder in the Basement* Roger frankly confesses that he uses real people in his books: "One always does that, in spite of the law of libel and the funny little notices some people put in the front of their books to say that all the characters in this story are imaginary. . . . Nobody could imagine a character and make it live."[47]

ABC/Berkeley gives us very little information about Sheringham's personal relationships. There are indications that he is keen on Anne Manners in *The Silk Stocking Murders,* he is briefly attracted to Sheila Purefoy in *The Wychford Poisoning Case*, and he actually courts and proposes to Stella Barnett in *Top Storey Murder.* (He professes to be intensely relieved when she turns him down.) Otherwise, he is a determined bachelor, well known for his view that it is better not to marry at all. The unhealed scars of a love affair, which saw the "right woman" marry someone else, perhaps explain his misogynist attitudes. At Wychford, he labels women "charming, delightful, adorable, but idiots" (although, after becoming temporarily smitten with Sheila, he laments that they can never be such "unutterable idiots" as men). He applies his estimate of the average woman's intelligence to the gullible Mrs Saunderson at Wychford, and sets out—unashamedly—to charm information out of her. He has no doubt he will succeed ("Good Lord, you talk as if the woman didn't want love made to her"), and her response justifies his confidence.

It is an understatement to say that Sheringham has a very high opinion of his own abilities. "I might be wrong," he concedes in *The Layton Court Mystery*, "but I very seldom am." He never loses faith in his sixth sense, and on occasion his instincts and insights do him credit. He proves to be cool-headed and quick-thinking in a crisis, as in *Panic Party* where he displays resource-fulness and leadership on Mr Pidgeon's island. Despite a couple of spectacular successes, and an intelligent and imaginative (sometimes over-imaginative) approach to solving crime, how-ever, Sheringham's accuracy as an investigator is erratic. His method springs out of his "eager curiosity regarding his fellow creatures, their minds and the passions which sway them." For Roger, the chief interest of a murder case is the people involved— the circumstances of the killing, the method, reasons and steps taken to elude detection. (In his view, the Thompson-Bywaters case, for instance, would have been just another sordid triangle were it not for the psychological element.) This reliance on psy-chology frequently misleads him. Fellow-members of the Crime Circle scoff at his view that some suspects cannot be guilty because of the psychological improbability. (What, they ask, about precedents where improbable people have done improbable things, for example, Lizzie Borden, Adelaide Bartlett or Con-stance Kent?) Sheringham's original solution to *The Wychford Poi-soning Case*, based on character, is ultimately displaced by a more prosaic one based on evidence. Sometimes he gets the answer half-right—at others, he is simply wrong. (Strickland notes that this fallibility becomes "a large part of the entertainment value of the novels; seeing how Roger is misled this time.")[48] Significantly, the perceptive Cyril Pinkerton enlists his help, in *The Second Shot*, because he knows Roger is clever enough to divert police suspi-cion from him, but not clever enough to discover that he (Pinker-ton) is really guilty!

Like ABC, Sheringham believes that the psychological aspects of true-life murders like the Crippen, Thompson and Seddon cases make them infinitely more fascinating than their fictional counterparts; his interest in them prompts him to found the Crime Circle. He has no doubt that a huge number of murders (particularly poisonings) are never discovered; while he has no evidence for his theory that one out of every 20 people is an undetected killer, he enjoys trying to pick out the 20th one. As he says to Alec in *The Layton Court Mystery*, there is nothing inherently improbable about murder. It is a common enough event; it just doesn't generally take place within one's immediate circle.

Roger is a devotee of the French method of reconstructing a crime. By successfully using Anne Manners as a decoy to trap the perpetrator of *The Silk Stocking Murders*, he believes he has proved the superiority of the inductive method of investigation. However, by *Top Storey Murder*, he has become aware of the dangers of forming one's theory first and then twisting certain awkward facts into confirmation of it. He breaks down Stella Barnett's alibi, and accuses her of the murder of her aunt, only to find that his inquiries have enabled Moresby to prove a case against someone quite different. Similarly, in "White Butterfly," he is so busy analyzing the character of the chief suspect that he misses out on the real murderer (although his deductions direct the police to the killer). Roger learns to appreciate the value of a partnership with Moresby, one which combines his own psychological and inductive style and the policeman's preference for routine leg-work and the dominant clue. Strickland notes: "Though Sheringham greatly prefers the armchair method, his acquaintance with the methodical, demanding Inspector Moresby . . . often makes the more active approach necessary."[49]

Notwithstanding the single-minded zest with which he is wont to attack an investigation, Roger has his own code of ethics. He refuses to investigate the Roland House mystery for Moresby because he knows all the suspects—"an amateur detective may have few standards left, but I haven't come down to spying on my friends yet." He does go down to the school to satisfy his own curiosity, however. On this occasion, his reliance on psychological probabilities is vindicated, but he allows the killer to go free because of the likely ramifications on the innocent should he act.

Sheringham is convinced that murder can be justified under certain circumstances. In both *Jumping Jenny* and *The Second Shot*, he believes the world is well rid of the victim, and he manufactures evidence to ensure no one is arrested. "I consider that I'm very much more competent than are twelve thick-headed rustics, presided over by a somnolent and tortuous-minded gentleman in an out-of-date wig," he declares. In "Perfect Alibi" he regrets that a respectable policeman felt compelled to suicide after justifiably eliminating an obnoxious libertine. ("By ridding the world of the man who betrayed his daughter, he did more good than he knew.") Roger is invariably exhilarated by the challenge of finding out whodunit, but his interest generally remains academic. "For heaven's sake . . . *do* try not to be so disgustingly conventional" is his reaction when the Layton Court culprit suggests taking himself off to the police. Interestingly, he is distinctly unhappy when he is suspected of murder himself (in *Jumping Jenny*), and he subsequently empathizes with the feelings of the "wretched murderer" whom Mr Pidgeon threatens to expose in *Panic Party*. In view of his previous affiliations with Scotland Yard, Sheringham takes responsibility for investigating Pidgeon's death but, once again, he is content to allow the culprit (a war hero) to evade the law.

The multiple solution and compound surprise ending are distinctive, readily identifiable characteristics of most of Anthony Berkeley Cox's crime-writing (as both Iles and Berkeley), and they are fundamental to the standard plot pattern of the Roger Sheringham novels. Dorothy L. Sayers, who held her colleague's work in high esteem (particularly "The Avenging Chance" and *The Poisoned Chocolates Case*), once summed up the formula: "There's the Roger Sheringham method, for instance. You prove elaborately and in detail that A did the murder; then you give the story one final shake, twist it round a fresh corner, and find that the real murderer is B—the person you suspected first and then lost sight of."[50]

More often than not, the diehard Berkeley enthusiast can guess the culprit, thanks to the author's tendency to introduce him/her at virtually the same point in each book. Yet the predictability detracts very little from the novels' overall effectiveness. It is more than made up for by ABC/Berkeley's sardonic humor, his diverting dissertations on crime and criminals (fictional and otherwise), and his considerable skill in characterization. Roger, in particular, is an ably delineated figure whose personality becomes increasingly complex in the course of the series.

Sheringham begins his detecting career as "a completely undisciplined and unconventional version of E.C. Bentley's Philip

Trent" (to quote Charles Shibuk), and finishes up giving a reasonably accurate impression of the conventional, traditional detective
hero.[51] Some of his rough edges are smoothed out in the process:
his initial offensiveness is played down, he becomes rather less
garrulous and more prepared to compromise in his investigating
style. Even so, he remains sublimely self-confident and entertain-
ingly and refreshingly fallible to the end.

5

ANTHONY BERKELEY (II):
MORESBY, CHITTERWICK AND OTHERS

The fallible but irrepressible Roger Sheringham remains ABC's most important and popular contribution to the classical detective story, but the Berkeley books and stories also feature a couple of other significant recurring investigators. As I noted in the previous chapter, Alec Grierson plays Watson to Roger's Holmes in the first two Sheringham cases (as well as the short story "Double Bluff"/"Direct Evidence") and, it turns out, holds the solution to the Layton Court slaying. The personable (if rather dim) Alec marries his fiancée, Barbara Shannon, in the interim between the two books, settles into untroubled domesticity in Dorset after the rigors of the Wychford investigation, and (at last mention) is said to be farming in Brazil.[1] Perhaps ABC/Berkeley recognized the limitations inherent in continually teaming Sheringham with an amateur offsider, and so dispensed with Grierson. He does allow Roger to enlist nonprofessionals in subsequent cases (Anthony Walton, Anne Manners and Lawrence Pleydell, for instance) but, from *The Vane Mystery* on, Sheringham's primary detecting relationship is with Moresby, a fully fledged and accredited policeman.

Moresby matches wits with Sheringham in five books and three short stories (plus the Sayers parody in *Ask a Policeman*); he also appears in *The Piccadilly Murder* (1929) and *Trial and Error* (1937), both of which feature Berkeley's second amateur sleuth, the mild and inoffensive Mr Chitterwick, and he makes a very brief cameo appearance in the radio play "Red Anemones," published in *The Roger Sheringham Stories* in 1994. (Moresby is teamed with both Chitterwick and Sheringham in one book, *The Poisoned Chocolates Case*.) As Berkeley, ABC also published two novels and three short stories which do not include any of his series characters, and he collaborated with fellow members of the Detection Club in four round-robin exercises. In addition to the unpublished Roger Sheringham material described in the previous chapter, the ABC archive (the basis for Johns's bibliography) contains several Berkeley manuscripts, including one completed novel.

Chief Inspector Moresby

Moresby makes his first appearance in *The Vane Mystery* when he descends on the coastal town of Ludmouth to look more closely into a suspicious "accidental death." He is described as a genial man who invariably presents an affable (and unflappable) exterior to the world. Indeed, it is suggested that he gets most of his results by exploiting his natural "kindness of disposition." Distinctively "ordinary" in behavior and appearance, burly, with stumpy, insensitive fingers and a grizzled moustache (which makes him look like a "benevolent walrus"), Moresby bears little outward likeness to the detective supermen of fiction. "His face resembled anything but a razor, or even a hatchet . . . his eyes had never been known to snap since infancy; and he simply never rapped out remarks—he just spoke them."[2] He is married with two children; otherwise we are given virtually no personal details about him. (We do not even know the Chief Inspector's first name.) He has a reputation as "one of the big noises at Scotland Yard," mixed up in every major murder case "for the last ten years." With Moresby on the scene (reasons Roger), something important is likely to be afoot.

Well-read, level-headed and intelligent, with an extensive knowledge of criminal history, Moresby is a talented and committed policeman, and a devout believer in orthodox methods of investigation. He argues that the solution to 99 percent of murder cases depends on patient and painstaking police legwork and deduction rather than any fanciful theorizing. Confronted with Sheringham's enthusiasm for the psychological approach, he maintains that "it's our business to deal with facts not fancies." Moresby would usually prefer to back evidence against "all the psychology in the world." He gleefully demolishes Sheringham's solution to *The Vane Mystery* (a gloriously speculative hypothesis that the two unsavory victims could have eliminated each other!); the Chief Inspector insists that the case was (and always had been) simplicity itself, that the most likely person had been quite obviously guilty all along, and that only the lack of concrete proof had forestalled police action. "No good detective ought to have too much imagination," he triumphs, suggesting that Sheringham has read too many detective stories.

Above all else however, the Chief Inspector is a seeker after truth, and he acknowledges that the assistance of amateurs like Sheringham or Chitterwick may be valuable on those (rare) occasions when the police are baffled or have their hands tied. Sheringham has his revenge for the Ludmouth humiliation when he beats the police at their own game and tracks down the perpetrator of *The Silk Stocking Murders*—"all," he exults, "by the inductive methods you people [Scotland Yard] don't use." ("You don't read enough of those detective stories" is his parting shot to Moresby.) By this stage though, a mutual respect has developed between professional and amateur; an intermittent partnership, nurtured by friendly rivalry, grows out of the silk stocking investigation. Moresby enjoys layman Roger's company and hospitality (not least the culinary skills of Meadows, his valet); the two men dine together once or twice a month, which gives them the opportunity to mull over cases currently puzzling Scotland Yard. The policeman recognizes that Sheringham's unofficial status enables him to go where officialdom cannot because of red tape or lack of evidence. In both "White Butterfly" and "The Wrong Jar," Moresby is intrigued by a possible village murder and miscarriage of justice, but professional etiquette precludes his becoming actively involved. Therefore he subtly persuades Sheringham to look into the matter. Similarly (and notwithstanding his professed scorn for "psychological fiddle-faddle"), he is not averse to employing psychology himself to induce an uncharacteristically reluctant Roger to probe into possible evildoings at his old prep school (in *Murder in the Basement*).

Moresby's method cleverly exploits his colleague's vanity—Sheringham relishes opportunities to "show old Moresby a thing or two." On his part, the Chief Inspector is not above letting Sheringham become involved in an investigation simply so he can demonstrate the superiority of orthodox police technique. In *Top Storey Murder* Moresby believes that an elderly woman's death is a straightforward case of burglary gone wrong, and one which bears the identifying trademarks of a small number of known criminals. Overimaginative Roger predictably finds incongruities in the case, but Moresby proves to be correct. The Chief Inspector has the grace to thank Sheringham for collating the evidence which will enable the police to arrest their original suspect; he is mercifully unaware that Sheringham had quite accurately established the circumstances of the killing—but in a bid to pin the murder on the wrong person. Nor does Roger enlighten him. (A similar twist occurs in "White Butterfly.")

On other occasions, Moresby is objective enough to recognize that Sheringham's inductive methods might have their uses. When the police give up hope of solving the poisoned chocolates murder, and can only postulate that an unknown homicidal maniac must be responsible, the Chief Inspector places the problem before Roger (in "The Avenging Chance") and the combined forces of the Crime Circle (in *The Poisoned Chocolates Case*). He is glowingly appreciative of Mr Chitterwick's solution (in the latter). Indeed, the self-effacing little man becomes something of a police pet at Scotland Yard (unlike Sheringham) and subsequently justifies Moresby's faith in him by solving *The Piccadilly Murder* and helping ensure that an innocent man does not hang in *Trial and Error*.

As a character, Moresby's main function in the Berkeley novels is to provide a quasi-realistic counterweight to Roger Sheringham's irreverent and wildly intuitive mode of investigation. Although he solves both *The Vane Mystery* and the *Top Storey Murder*, the Chief Inspector's deductive work remains secondary to the main detection in all but one of the books. (His appearances in *Trial and Error* are only fleeting.) The exception is *Murder in the Basement*, in which the author goes into considerable detail describing police efforts to establish the identity of a woman buried in a suburban cellar. This uncharacteristically serious Berkeley novel deliberately deglamorizes police procedure, and contains grimly realistic descriptions of the state of the corpse (buried several months) and graphic detail of medical analysis. In attempting to discover just how the unknown victim came to be buried in that particular London basement, Moresby and his colleagues are forced to sift through a mountain of missing persons reports and medical records. The fortuitous presence of a steel plate in the woman's leg finally enables the police to trace the victim to a preparatory school in the country. Only then does Sheringham become involved—by the sheerest coincidence he had recently deputized for a sick friend at the school, and so had a firsthand knowledge of its inhabitants. Of course, the twist to the book (which seems to celebrate the reality of plodding police procedure over amateur meddling) is that, for once, it is Sheringham who uncovers the true culprit—thanks to his reliance on the psychological approach!

Mr Chitterwick

The erratic Sheringham and "ordinary" Moresby are both conscious departures from the stereotype of the Great Detective and, as such, both were innovations in 1920s crime fiction. ABC/Berkeley subsequently offered readers yet another alternative when he introduced the mild-mannered Mr Ambrose Chitterwick (a timid amateur who was "everything which Holmes or even Roger was not") in *The Poisoned Chocolates Case*.[3] Indeed (to quote Charles Shibuk), the "ineffectual and astute" Chitterwick is the "complete antithesis" of Sheringham.[4] We first meet him pondering unhappily on how to go about tracking down Joan Bendix's killer; he has always attempted to live quietly and at peace with his neighbors ("no one can do that and be a detective as well"), and so finds himself at a loss when called upon to play detective.

He had studied the reminiscences of a hundred ex-detectives, the real ones, with large black boots and bowler hats; but all he could remember at that moment, out of all those scores of fat books . . . was that a real, *real* detective, if he means to attain results, never puts on a false moustache but simply shaves his eyebrows. As a mystery-solving formula, this seemed to Mr Chitterwick inadequate.[5]

It comes as no surprise to the reader, of course, that the little man overcomes his initial distaste for active detecting and proceeds to beat more experienced (and more likely) criminologists at their own game.

The three books which feature the self-effacing Mr Chitterwick are (arguably) ABC's finest achievements under his Anthony Berkeley alias. Apart from *The Poisoned Chocolates Case*, which I discussed in the previous chapter (and in which he provides the solution to a puzzle that has eluded both Scotland Yard and several illustrious nonprofessionals), Chitterwick is at the center of the action in *The Piccadilly Murder* and figures significantly (if less prominently) in *Trial and Error.*

In the opening chapter of *The Piccadilly Murder*, a well-to-do elderly lady takes afternoon tea with her nephew (and heir) in the crowded lounge of a leading London hotel; they argue, the nephew leaves and she dies. (Her coffee has been laced with prussic acid.) Mr Chitterwick happens to be seated only a few tables away, and the police are able to charge the nephew on his evidence. The situation is not as clear-cut as it seems. When Chitterwick is enticed to a house-party in the country, he finds himself surrounded by friends and relatives of the accused, all of them insistent the man is innocent and that he (Chitterwick) rethink his evidence. He finally yields and agrees to "look into the matter," aided by the alleged killer's attractive wife and a young duke who answers to the nickname Mouse. Eventually Chitterwick uncovers a clever conspiracy involving multiple impersonations, and he successfully identifies the real murderer and motive.

The Piccadilly Murder is a lighthearted and still highly enjoyable novel, distinguished by its clever plotting, the author's sometimes caustic asides, and the perspicacity of the unlikely but likeable sleuth. Apart from Chitterwick, the book's characters are a stock Golden Age mix of one-dimensional middle-class Londoners and country gentry (neither victim, suspect nor killer excites much interest); however, there is one glorious exception, the reticent little investigator has a wonderfully formidable aunt. The comic interplay between this terrifying relative and her put-upon nephew remains one of the highlights of the Berkeley books. Another of *The Piccadilly Murder*'s delights is the scene of the crime—the vast "gilt and synthetic-marble" hotel lounge which Dale and Hendershott identify as the main dining room and carvery of the Regent Palace Hotel near Piccadilly Circus.[6] Visitors to London can still take afternoon tea amid the imitation marble pillars and art deco plushness which inspired ABC/Berkeley to write: "To us who frequent it the Piccadilly Palace is what Monte Carlo is to Europe's new rich, our pride, our Mecca and our rendezvous."[7]

As Strickland points out, *Trial and Error* "adopts the conventions of the detective story only to turn them inside-out," and it represents a major departure from the previous Berkeley cases.[8] Much closer to the "inverted" novels of character ABC wrote as Francis Iles than to the Sheringham books, only the strong vein of humor and the presence of Moresby and Chitterwick, distinguish it as a Berkeley novel. We are aware of the would-be murderer's identity and motivation from the start, just as we are in Iles's *Malice Aforethought* and *Before the Fact*. In *Trial and Error*, however, multiple twists add an extra and unexpected dimension to the denouement (recalling the conclusion of *Jumping Jenny*).

Trial and Error's hero is the terminally ill Lawrence Butterfield Todhunter, who decides he will benefit humanity and rid the world of some worthless, destructive parasite before he dies himself. Ruling out annihilating Mussolini or Hitler (as unfeasible), the genial Todhunter first selects an offensive publisher but is beaten to the post by someone else. Todhunter settles therefore for Jean Norwood, a thoroughly poisonous actress. The rest of the novel details his increasingly frantic bids to prove his own guilt when one of Norwood's young playthings is convicted of the crime. In the face of Scotland Yard's skepticism (Moresby believes he is a lunatic), Todhunter enlists Chitterwick to find clues which will connect him with the killing. A civil trial for murder is initiated and Todhunter is ultimately found guilty, but his terminal condition enables him to cheat the gallows at the eleventh hour.

Shibuk has dubbed *Trial and Error* easily the best of the Berkeley novels, and second only to Iles's *Before the Fact*, while Strickland judges it ABC's finest opus "in either of his criminous incarnations. . . . It is a mad tea-party of a book, with the inverted form combined with the puzzle, the courtroom drama with near farce, the novel of suspense with the comedy of P.G. Wodehouse."[9] The book attracted generally favorable reviews on its release although there was some carping about its length (it is almost twice as long as most of the Sheringham novels), and the legal complexities of the plot elicited considerable discussion. ABC later defended himself against accusations that his law was "pretty poor"; he pointed out that *Trial and Error* drew its inspiration from the Serafino Pelizzioni case (1866), in which the perpetrator of a street killing (for which another man had been convicted) found himself unable to convince the police of his guilt. The only solution for him was a private prosecution for murder which resulted in both men languishing in jail for the same crime while authority scratched its head and sought a way out of the impasse. Given this stranger-than-fiction precedent, ABC countered that his law was indeed "pretty good." Certainly the incident provided him with a remarkable and brilliantly executed plot.[10] (ABC reexamined the Pelizzioni case with a radio play in the 1950s.)[11]

Compared with his prominence in *The Piccadilly Murder*, Chitterwick is a distinctly secondary presence in *Trial and Error*, but he displays his mettle once again when he helps prove the case against Todhunter and thus saves the luckless Vincent Palmer. Chitterwick seems to hold the key to the mystery at the book's conclusion. He realizes that Todhunter had been innocent all along but, in the type of ironic afterword with which ABC excels, Chitterwick also turns out to have been misled (quite uncharacteristically). In the end neither Todhunter nor Chitterwick is ever aware that a further unknown factor has been at play.

Panek has noted the strong kinship between Chitterwick and other self-effacing and deceptively insignificant little men in the ABC and Berkeley books: the beleaguered hero of *Mr Priestley's Problem*, the narrator of *Not to Be Taken*, the altruistic Mr Todhunter in *Trial and Error*, and *The Second Shot*'s Cyril Pinkerton. Each of them can be described as "eternal victim"—easily intimidated, naive, ignored or overlooked by more hardy beings, and often the target of "loud, insensitive, hearty souls like [Sheringham]."[12] Ironically, each one reveals unsuspected capacities under pressure, and ultimately emerges triumphant. It is tempting to speculate also on parallels between Chitterwick and ABC.

Just as Roger Sheringham shared a number of biographical commonalities with his creator, and undeniably served as his mouthpiece on questions of law, literature and society, Mr Chitterwick seems to have been endowed with aspects of ABC's outlook and personality, even his appearance. As a partial self-portrait, along the lines of Christie's Mrs Ariadne Oliver or (perhaps) Sayers's Harriet Vane, Chitterwick shares (and articulates) identifiably Coxian sentiments. "What is justice?" he queries when confronted with the ethical dilemma raised by Todhunter's actions in

Trial and Error. "They say murder can never be justified. But can't it? Is human life so valuable that it is better to preserve a pestilential nuisance alive rather than bring happiness to a great many persons by eliminating one? . . . Todhunter did not shirk it. I can't say I don't think he was right."[13] Although he is distressed by the notion of a dying man committing an altruistic killing, Chitterwick concedes that it may be for the best. When it is suggested that a particularly unattractive newspaper tycoon would be better out of the way because of his deliberate deception of his readers, Chitterwick asks ("with unwonted cynicism"), "Wouldn't that mean all newspaper proprietors?" Chitterwick also shares ABC's fascination with criminology and the low opinion of statesmen which the writer verbalized in *O England*.

The description of Chitterwick as a "red-faced, somewhat globular, early middle aged gentleman of independent means, with a gold-rimmed pince-nez on a very short nose," bears an unmistakable resemblance to the caricature George Morrow drew of ABC for the frontispiece of *Jugged Journalism*. Similarly, the name (Ambrose Chitterwick) is an obvious parallel. Elsewhere, the author notes that his alter ego has "mild blue eyes," a cherubic face, and the appearance of "an intelligent nanny-goat."[14] He attributes Chitterwick's "remarkable mildness" to the little man's domestic situation—and specifically, his "extremely ancient aunt" who rules him with a rod "something stronger than iron." Like her early Jacobean house in Chiswick, Miss Chitterwick (aged 79, and likely to live to 100) is described as an anachronism. The sole owner of her property, "in every sense of the word an aunt," she has been waited on by her nephew since he was 30. (At the time of the Piccadilly Palace case he is 44.) He succeeded his three sisters (all now married) and, although Miss Chitterwick grumbles because he is not a girl, he has proved to be the best companion, errand-boy and dogsbody of them all. Experience has taught him to take the line of least resistance with the old lady—in fact, he deems himself quite content with her, his stamp collection and his interest in criminology. He rarely finds the company of strangers congenial but he is honored to be included in Sheringham's Crime Circle; he is also a keen member of the Royal Horticultural Society. He is known to indulge a quiet fondness for claret or a good sherry on occasion, and has just treated himself to an after-coffee

Benedictine when he witnesses Miss Sinclair's murder in the Piccadilly Palace lounge.

"A modest student of the human animal," Chitterwick counterbalances his mildness and subservience to his aunt with his hobby. He has made the study of true crime his ruling passion ever since he first visited Madame Tussaud's Chamber of Horrors at age nine. He knows the names, dates, stories, psychology, color of eyes, almost the number of teeth, of every murderer of even minor importance since Alice Arden of Faversham (in 1551). Chitterwick collects murderers as lesser souls collect moths, sticking "psychological pins through their inmost recesses" and spreading them out on card indexes and cross-files. One of his favorite pastimes is a mental game of "Detectives," in which he tries to deduce the histories of people he sees around him; he invariably plays it on the Underground to Chiswick, and it is this game which first brings the Piccadilly Palace victim to his notice. He is both horrified and thrilled by his first real-life encounter with murder.

Chitterwick's solution to the poisoned chocolates murder goes unpublicized, and the case is necessarily written off as unsolvable. In contrast to Sheringham, the little man's modesty prevents him from believing that any great credit accrues to him anyway. He maintains that he simply used the results garnered by his more adventurous colleagues to come up with the truth, and that anyone of moderate intelligence might have done the same. His skill earns him official congratulations from the Scotland Yard chiefs, and *The Piccadilly Murder* exposes him to a degree of press notice, but his incursions into crime have little material impact on his way of life. (Panek notes that Chitterwick never gets the girl, "persistently refuses the limelight," and goes back to "his obscure retirement and dowdy respectability" at the end of each case.)[15] The praise of Chief Inspector Moresby and the press do fortify him to effect a minor revolution at home though. After the Piccadilly Palace case he insists that his aunt employ a professional companion, and *Trial and Error* finds him in proud possession of his own sitting room and a telephone. Most importantly, his aunt has developed a grudging admiration for his ability. When Todhunter tells her of his concern that an innocent man could well hang for the murder he had committed, she might scoff ("Well, the noospapers call Ambrose a detective nowadays, it seems. I suppose they don't know what a guffin he is"), but it is she who suggests that Chitterwick detect Todhunter's murder for him. Perhaps this is the greatest accolade the henpecked Mr Chitterwick could wish for.

Other Anthony Berkeley Publications

Trial and Error, the final Chitterwick book, was also the last of the Berkeley novels to feature one or other of the author's recurring investigators. ABC subsequently published two non-series Berkeley novels, both conscientious examples of the classical puzzle story (although they are rendered above the average by the writer's characteristic wit and satiric bent). Three non-series Berkeley short stories were also published in the 1930s.

The novels were originally written as serials for *John O'London's Weekly*. Both make a point of playing fair with the evidence; the author pauses formally just before all is revealed and invites the reader to guess whodunit, how and why, on the basis of the clues provided. *Not to Be Taken* (1938; in the United States *A Puzzle in Poison*) is a straightforward tale of poisoning, set in a traditionally cosy, Christie-style English village (the fictional Anneypenny in Dorset). Like *The Wychford Poisoning Case*, it draws on the Maybrick murder, and duplicates that famous case's *dramatis personae*: philandering victim, faithless wife, vengeful brother-in-law, spiteful housemaid. John Waterhouse, a prosperous engineer/industrialist, is being treated by the local G.P. for what appears to be an incipient gastric ulcer. He dies unexpectedly following a particularly severe bout of indigestion, and subsequent inquiries reveal traces of arsenic in his system. Waterhouse's widow becomes the police's prime suspect, but there are other possibilities: a revenge-killing by one of the man's discarded mistresses, a possible dispensing error by the rather inept doctor, even espionage. (Waterhouse turns out to have been working undercover for British Intelligence.)

The book's narrator is Douglas Sewell, a neighbor of the murdered man, who turns amateur detective and successfully identifies and confronts the killer. Another of ABC's apparent weaklings, Sewell is a reasonably intelligent man, very conservative (public school) in his language and politics, undemonstrative, and afflicted with a mild inferiority complex. He solves the case but then faces an ethical dilemma over what action he should or should not take. (Ultimately, we assume, he does nothing.)

By far the most interesting character in *Not to Be Taken* is the local doctor's sister, Rona Brougham, an Oxford-educated feminist and the village's resident intellectual. Energetic, forceful, considerably more capable then her brother, Rona's no-nonsense approach to life encompasses a radical conception of law and justice. She advocates the humane elimination of habitual criminals, "useless nuisances" and criminal lunatics, but disapproves of punishment for the average person. ("Punishment does more harm than good," she reasons. "It's barbarous. An eye for an eye, a tooth for a tooth, a life for a life, eh? I'm afraid you're terribly Old Testament, Douglas.") Rona echoes Mr Todhunter in her belief that ridding the world of a worthless person is not in itself a criminal act. Why, she asks, should a useful member of society be exterminated for having got rid of a useless member?[16]

To a stunned Sewell, this sounds like "sheer Bolshevism," and certainly Rona's pronouncements are disconcerting when we remember that *Not to Be Taken* was written in the late 1930s. To what extent she is a spokesperson for the author's viewpoint here is difficult to assess. The book contains numerous references to Germany and the European situation, and two of the murder victim's servants turn out to be Nazi sympathizers (in the guise of Austrian refugees). An astute old lady observes to Sewell: "The Germans have no sense of humour about themselves. It makes me doubt very much whether they can really come from the same stock as ourselves."[17] Elsewhere, ABC/Berkeley effectively lampoons Nazi fanaticism in the comic character of Maria Pfeiffer, a massive, incompetent cook (and rabid Fascist) who complacently dismisses all her critics as "Chews."

Not to Be Taken is a well-written, skillfully constructed detective story which earned deservedly favorable reviews (although one or two critics argued that the murderer's motivation was out of character).[18] The last Berkeley book, *Death in the House* (1939), was less successful. The author again gave a nod to topical international developments, this time the Indian Independence movement. The setting is the House of Commons where members of Britain's Conservative Government are attempting to introduce its highly contentious India Bill. According to the Government, the legislation aims to curb misguided separatists from "murdering, pillaging or burning the persons or property" of other Indian citizens; its passage is violently opposed by pro-Independence forces at home and abroad.

Despite a series of anonymous death threats, the Secretary of State for India insists on speaking to the bill in Parliament; he collapses on the floor of the House and dies shortly after. The same thing happens when his successor attempts to introduce the bill. Medical examination indicates that both men have been killed by the South American arrow poison curare, and it is clear that the culprit must be someone in the Chamber. A prominent financier, with massive investments in India, is killed in a similar fashion, the India Office is bombed, a junior civil servant is shot, and yet another Cabinet member is poisoned in the House before the culprit is apprehended.

Death in the House is somewhat flawed, and suggests that the author may well have exhausted his capacity or inclination to write mystery puzzles of this sort. The Parliamentary setting is well done but most of the characters fail to come to life, and the dialogue is uncharacteristically tedious in places. Lord Arthur Linton, the Under-secretary of State for India, who functions as amateur sleuth, is a decidedly uninteresting young man; he does redeem himself somewhat, however, by seizing the initiative, frantically delivering the long-awaited speech at the novel's climax, and narrowly avoiding his predecessors' fate in the process. This suspenseful conclusion is the best part of the book, even though the means of injecting the poison into the various victims proves to be rather too far-fetched. ABC's contemporary, Nicholas Blake, called the book "badly overpitched," and criticized the murder method as "so fanciful that a schoolboy could crack it for six." Barzun and Taylor have suggested that Berkeley was "more adept with poisoned chocolates."[19]

Where *Death in the House* continues to entertain the reader best is in the author's incisive (often cynical) assessment of British politics and society of the 1930s. Presumably we are hearing ABC's own exasperation with statesmen (cf. *O England*) when the leaders of Government are likened to a parish council, met to decide a question concerning the parish pump. Hardly one of them is said to be fit for anything more than the duties of rural justice of the peace or church-warden. ("Just facade—and behind it nothing but wind. Were these really the best that the country could produce, to govern it.")[20] Nor are politicians the only targets. More than one character laments "the deadly, dull, complacent indifference of the British public," and fear is expressed that E.M. Forster's picture of British civil servants (in *A Passage to India*) may not have been an exaggeration. The press is also given a serve; the pro-Labour papers blame the House of Commons murders on "our policy of non-intervention in Spain," and declare that it would serve the Government right if the Cabinet were to be killed off, man by man: "Obviously, any Government which could apply force to anyone or anything or upon any excuse (except, of course, the persons or things against which the Opposition newspapers themselves wished to employ force, that is to say, any foreigner who did not happen to hold their own political opinions) must deserve the dread label Fascist."[21]

The first of three non-series short stories by Berkeley was "Mr Simpson Goes to the Dogs," which appeared in *The Strand* in June 1934. Its protagonist, Mr Horace Simpson, is a nondescript but officious bank cashier, a somewhat less endearing variant of Priestley, Pinkerton and Chitterwick. Visiting the greyhound races out of curiosity, Simpson sees what he believes to be a girl pickpocket in action. His attempt to intercept her triggers a series of misadventures which culminate in his own arrest, but in a typical Berkeley volte-face, he ends up with a sizeable reward for helping the police recover some stolen emeralds.

In 1936 ABC contributed Berkeley stories to two collections. *Missing from Their Homes* cashed in on the popularity of radio broadcasts about missing persons, with such well-known writers as Graham Greene, E.M. Delafield, Louis Golding and Arthur Machen contributing serious or comic short stories on the theme of disappearance. Berkeley's "Publicity Heroine" was a broad farce which mixed up the British nobility with New York's gangland (a la Wodehouse). A madcap society girl, Lady Felicia Cowes-Banneret, enlists a couple of minor New York gangsters to help stage her own kidnapping (as a publicity stunt). She is understandably miffed when the inept pair double-cross her, confine her to a cellar and demand a huge ransom from her father and the British Government; Lady Felicia is even less pleased when it becomes clear that no one is particularly interested in getting her back. In due course, she finds herself smitten with one of the gangsters (tough-guy Joe Magaretti), whose rudeness and indifference she finds irresistible. She readily marries him and their knockabout public appearances win her more publicity then she ever dreamed of. However, the alliance and its attendant notoriety prove distinctly embarrassing to Lady Felicia's baronet father, who welcomes the pair's timely deportation back to the United States (as undesirable aliens).[22]

The second collection was a Detection Club anthology, *Six Against the Yard* (in the United States, *Six Against Scotland Yard*), in which ABC, Dorothy L. Sayers, Margery Allingham, Freeman Wills Crofts, Ronald Knox and Russell Thorndike each attempted to devise a murder plot clever enough to fool professional policemen. Ex-Superintendent Cornish of the C.I.D. was on hand to scrutinize each case and provide a written critique. The Berkeley story again explored the comic possibilities of the American underworld: "The Policeman Only Taps Once" was a delightful parody of James Cain and the "hardboiled" school of crime writing—with, perhaps, a tongue-in-cheek dig at ABC himself (in his Francis Iles guise) in the opening paragraph. ("It was a dull sort of day, cloudy and raw like they get it over here, so I thought I'd bump off Myrtle. She had it coming to her anyway.")[23] A Yankee con man, on vacation from the States ("for his health"), aims "to find some old dame who'd got dough of her own and a face like the back-view of a cab-horse, and marry her." He entraps an apparently well-to-do spinster only to discover that she has been playing a similar con game with him. "Eddie" schemes to get rid of his wife via a convenient bathroom explosion but foolishly puts his plan in writing. Myrtle finds out and breezily adapts the method to ensure that it is her errant spouse who becomes the victim.

In addition to the published items cited above, the ABC archive contains a handful of non-series Berkeley typescripts, most notably three unpublished play scripts and a novel. "Man Proposes" is a one-act romantic dialogue, of no detective interest, and probably a very early effort (c. 1920). "Trial and Error" is a radio play based on the novel of the same name, and signed "by

Anthony Berkeley, adapted for broadcasting by Francis Iles."
Aired by the BBC on December 12, 1957, it was part of the "Con-
noisseurs of Crime" series for which famous crime-writers
selected and discussed their favorite cases. Another play, "The
Case of Serafino Pelizzioni," detailed the real-life case on which
ABC/Berkeley based *Trial and Error* and was broadcast the following week. (The archive also contains an incomplete dramatization
of the short story "Publicity Heroine." See note 22.)[24]

The novel, which is signed "by the author of *The Layton Court
Mystery*," is a Bulldog Drummond–style thriller called *An Amateur Adventuress*. It was obviously developed for serialization but
no trace of periodical publication has been found. The title character is "a spirited chorus girl" who falls into the clutches of a criminal gang and its leader, the "duke," after she witnesses a murder.
The plot details her exploits as she manages an escape and then
sets about unmasking the mysterious duke. Johns notes that the
story boasts a truly magnificent villainess, and that ABC/Berke-
ley's talent for set-piece situations (such as the young heroine's
capture and torture) is well in evidence.[25]

Detection Club Collaborations

Six Against The Yard was one of several team ventures by the
Detection Club. Also published in 1936 was *The Anatomy of
Murder*, in which writers dissected seven true murder mysteries. (I
look at the ABC/Iles analysis of the thought-provoking Rattenbury case in chapter 7.) As Berkeley, ABC also contributed to two
round-robin radio serials, *Behind the Screen* and *The Scoop*, and two
collaborative novels, *The Floating Admiral* and *Ask a Policeman.*

Early in 1930, J.R. Ackerley of the BBC's Talks Department
suggested that the Detection Club prepare a six-part radio serial,
with each contributor to read his/her installment on air. Members
welcomed the project as a means of raising funds for club
premises; accordingly, Ronald Knox, Hugh Walpole, Dorothy L.
Sayers, E.C. Bentley, Agatha Christie and ABC were recruited.
Walpole established the *mise en scene:* Wilfred Hope, a young
medical student, is becoming increasingly alarmed at the hold a
mysterious lodger seems to have over his fiancée and her family.
As the story begins, Wilfred is on his way to spend the evening
with the family; he finds them behaving quite naturally, but he

senses an underlying disquiet. The tension snaps when the lodger's body is discovered behind a screen in the drawing room.

Christie and Sayers developed and elaborated on Walpole's opening scene, then left it to their three successors to unravel the mystery, account logically for all the clues (and red herrings) and come up with a reasonable solution. The end-product, called *Behind the Screen*, was broadcast between June 14 and July 19, 1930, and each installment was published in the BBC's *Listener* the following week.[26] Milward Kennedy launched a competition in conjunction with the serial, calling on listeners to guess the identity and defense of the killer, and whether the death was accident, suicide or murder. ABC/Berkeley's contribution was episode 4, "In the Aspidistra" (broadcast July 5, published July 9), in which the murder weapon is located. The installment provides readers with a timetable summarizing the situation as seen by the investigator, Inspector Rice, and contains interviews with the various suspects (including the killer).

Notwithstanding technical problems with the BBC's unpredictable microphones, and the logistical difficulties of dovetailing each author's idiosyncratic contribution into a cohesive whole, the serial proved successful enough for the BBC to suggest a follow-up.[27] ABC and Sayers treated listeners to a duologue, "Plotting a Detective Story" (broadcast on July 23), in which they employed Sheringham and Lord Peter Wimsey to investigate a hypothetical electrocution in a bathtub; Sayers subsequently organized and coordinated a second, more ambitious serial, *The Scoop*, which aired for 12 weeks from January 10, 1932, and was again published in the *Listener*.[28] This time the participants were Sayers, Christie, Bentley, Freeman Wills Crofts, Clemence Dane and ABC. Each writer contributed two installments; ABC/Berkeley's were episodes 5 and 9, broadcast on February 14 and March 14 respectively.

The BBC's insistence on story-line simplicity, and the difficulty of just getting all the writers together at any one time, proved something of a headache for Sayers, but *The Scoop* turned out to be an advancement on *Behind the Screen*, partly by virtue of its greater length.[29] Johnson, a reporter for the *Morning Star* newspaper, goes down to Brighton to cover a sensational murder case and notifies his office that he has managed to locate the murder weapon (an oriental jade-headed pin). Johnson is killed in a phone booth at Victoria Station before he can give his editor any further details of the scoop; subsequent investigations by another reporter, Oliver, and the manager's secretary, Beryl Braidwood, uncover sinister links between the newspaper office and the two killings. In episode 5, "Tracing Tracey," Oliver seeks the missing chief suspect, and interviews several key witnesses. (He treats one, an "intensely blond" mannequin, to cocktails at the fashionable Piccadilly Palace Hotel.) One interviewee puts forward the intriguing theory that the missing man and the murdered reporter may well be the same man, and so establishes a connection between the cases. In episode 9, "Bond Street or Broad Street?" Beryl presents her deductions to her boss—a most unfortunate move. An unsuccessful attempt is made on her life in a later episode, but the culprit gets his just desserts at the conclusion, and the *Morning Star* revels in another scoop. Johns believes there may have been plans to expand the project into a book, as a typescript exists of Sayers's first installment which is much longer than that printed in the *Listener*. It was probably superseded by the Detection Club's first collaborative novel, *The Floating Admiral* (1931).[30]

The complexities of *The Floating Admiral* reflect the multiple talents involved, 14 writers in all: G.K. Chesterton, Victor Whitechurch, G.D.H. and M. Cole, Henry Wade, Agatha Christie, John Rhode, Milward Kennedy, Dorothy L. Sayers, Ronald Knox, Freeman Wills Crofts, Edgar Jepson, Clemence Dane and ABC. Inspector Rudge, "a quite ordinary man" who does not "solace himself with the violin, or the cocaine bottle . . . tie knots in string, or collect scarabs," is a policeman in the seacoast town of Whynmouth. He is called in to investigate when the corpse of Admiral Penistone is found floating down the river in the local vicar's dinghy. Suspects include the admiral's niece, her fiancé, the vicar, the local squire and a couple of mysterious strangers, all of whom appear to have something to hide. Why, for instance, do most of them race up to London as soon as the admiral's body is discovered? The story abounds in suspicious midnight meetings, bloodstained evening wear, impersonations and long-lost heirs. At one point, an elusive French maid reappears in Whynmouth only to die before she can reveal some crucial information; there is also a probable link with a minor scandal that occurred 20 years earlier in Hong Kong.

ABC was handed the unenviable task of tying all these strands together, and he did so most effectively. In his lengthy closing chapter, "Clearing Up the Mess," Inspector Rudge solves the mystery, disposes of the red herrings, establishes the significance of (among other things) a clump of valerian, and sees the killer behind bars (although the culprit expires before signing a confession). Sayers praised the "native ingenuity" with which ABC/Berkeley frustrated his colleagues' "knavish tricks" so adroitly, and the *Times Literary Supplement* judged: "Mr Anthony Berkeley performs such a remarkable feat of invisible mending that the story should wear quite well."[31]

Ask a Policeman (1933) employs a highly diverting gimmick. John Rhode sets the scene: Lord Comstock, a powerful newspaper magnate, notorious for his attacks on Christianity and Government policies, is shot dead at his country retreat. Suspicion falls in turn on his secretary, his butler, a mysterious lady visitor, the police, even an archbishop. Milward Kennedy provides the solution to the mystery in the final chapter, while in between, Dorothy L. Sayers, Helen Simpson, Gladys Mitchell and ABC investigate the case but swap their detectives to do so. (Sayers chronicles Sheringham's inquiries, ABC/Berkeley parodies Lord Peter Wimsey, Mitchell Sir John Saumarez, and Simpson Mrs Bradley.)

The result is a breezy, good-humored pastiche, undoubtedly the most entertaining of the Detection Club's collaborations. Certainly the writers appear to revel in sending up each others' pet sleuths. ABC/Berkeley's contribution "Lord Peter's Privy Counsel," gives us a delicious caricature of Sayers's Wimsey as a "silly ass," addicted to quotations, and preoccupied with the pleasures of the table. He insists on educating Inspector Parker in the niceties of gourmet eating, and expresses astonishment at the murdered man's vulgarity: ". . . with my own eyes I once saw him grab a piece of ginger after dinner and shove it into his beastly mouth just before taking his first sip of a '63 port." ("Shooting's a jolly sight too peaceful an end for a man who could do a thing like that," he judges.)[32] The parody encompasses stock Sayers characters such as Miss Climpson and the Dowager Duchess of Denver (although not Harriet Vane), and it provides a delightfully outrageous solution to the mystery (one more typical of ABC than Sayers to be sure): Wimsey deduces that the culprit is the Home Secretary, Sir Philip Brackenthorpe, the man who had recruited the assistance of the amateur investigators in the first place. Wimsey applauds Brackenthorpe's action as all for the national good, and notes that the Home Secretary enjoys the unique advantage of being able to reprieve himself!

The *Times Literary Supplement* carped that *Ask a Policeman* was rather a waste of so many "excellent plots and so much ingenuity" in a world "which needs detective fiction as an escape from reality"; otherwise critical reaction was positive: the exercise was variously judged "an amusing melange," an "amusing and worthwhile offering," and "not much of a detective story, but it is mighty good fooling."[33] Subsequently, various combinations of Detection Club members collaborated on a novel *Double Death* (1939), two more newspaper serials, *No Flowers by Request* (1953) and *Crime on the Coast* (1954), and a thematic short story anthology *Verdict of 13* (1978); ABC did not participate in any of these projects.

ABC's career as Anthony Berkeley grew out of his fondness for the traditional detective story, and he maintained his enthusiasm for the "straight-forward, honest-to-goodness puzzle" throughout his life.[34] As a creative artist however, he was not blind to the limitations of the genre and, indeed, he was responsible for a number of distinctive innovations which had a revitalizing impact, and highlighted (among other things) "how much fun an intelligent person can have with this crabbed and artificial form."[35] "Anyone with intelligence and something of a crossword puzzle mind can construct a competent detective story," he once observed, "but to keep the excitement piling up from chapter to chapter, to work up to an unforeseen climax through a succession of startling incidents, above all to keep close enough to real life to be credible and yet just that small distance outside it which the formula requires, all these require a range of talents, invention, and literary panache beside which the crossword mind sometimes looks desiccated and sterile."[36] His remarks were directed at two of his peers, Agatha Christie and Michael Gilbert, but they apply just as much to himself. From *The Layton Court Mystery* on, the

Anthony Berkeley novels and stories demonstrate the writer's superiority over the "humdrum" puzzle-writers of his day (to use Julian Symons's epithet). As well as nurturing such novel departures from the norm as multilayered surprise endings, multiple solutions, the triumph of plodding policemen over effervescent amateurs, and the frequent triumph of so-called natural justice over the law, the Berkeley products are distinguished by their humor, their incisive (often cynical) appraisal of British social mores and a zest and liveliness which (to quote Symons again) "keep them fresh even today."[37] Melvyn Barnes lauds ABC/Berkeley's talent for endowing shallow and superficial characters with enough "life" to make them credible; likewise, he praises the writer's distinctive ability to enact a moving character study and then "stun" the reader with a totally unpredictable outcome (*Trial and Error,* for instance).[38]

It appears however, that ABC felt he was on the way to exhausting the potential/possibilities of the puzzle-story (and of his irreverent variants on it) after *The Piccadilly Murder.* Johns suggests that his best work in the genre was behind him by the beginning of the 1930s,[39] and in the preface to *The Second Shot,* ABC wrote:

I personally am convinced that the days of the old crime puzzle pure and simple, relying entirely upon plot, and without any added attractions of character, style, or even humour, are, if not numbered, at any rate in the hands of the auditors . . . The puzzle element will no doubt remain, but it will become a puzzle of character rather than a puzzle of time, place, motive, and opportunity. The question will be, not, "*Who* killed the old man in the bathroom?" but, "What on earth induced X, of all people, to kill the old man in the bathroom?" . . . books will no longer end with the usual bald exposition of the detective in the last chapter. . . . In a word, the detective story must become more sophisticated.[40]

The Second Shot was, in fact, still a whodunit in which all was revealed in the last chapter (although with a slant which echoed Christie's *Murder of Roger Ackroyd*), but the sentiments expressed above foreshadowed the "inverted" crime novels written under the name of Francis Iles. ABC continued to write (relatively) standard whodunits (*Not to Be Taken, Top Storey Murder, Death in the House*) but this quest for a new direction in crime writing was felt in several of the later Berkeley books. Barzun and Taylor maintain that *Murder in the Basement* anticipates the police procedural subgenre by many years.[41] *Trial and Error* is essentially a novel of character, much closer to the Iles books than to the Sheringham cases. In *Jumping Jenny* we are seemingly shown a crime being committed and are privy to the perpetrator from that point on (although one of the author's more outrageous twists redefines the whole case). *Panic Party* balances a plot which conforms more to the thriller than to the whodunit with a rather disturbing study of an isolated and emotionally volatile group under duress. Thus, while ABC's Anthony Berkeley publications generally fall within the broad category of the formal puzzle-story, their range is somewhat greater than the label would suggest. For ABC's most radical reworking of the detective story though, we turn to his Francis Iles persona.

6

FRANCIS ILES

Like Agatha Christie, who penned romances as Mary Westmacott, ABC was a firm believer in the writer's need to employ pseudonyms when departing from the style in which he or she had attained popularity. "The reading public demands consistency in its authors," he wrote. "If Mr X, who has specialised in cosy suburbanism, gets an urge to write a stream-of-consciousness novel about a Siberian bird-watcher on Lake Chad, he must either suppress the impulse or unburden himself under another name."[1] With his Anthony Berkeley alias indelibly associated by the public with Roger Sheringham and the detective puzzle-story, he adopted a new *nom de plume*, Francis Iles, in tribute to his smuggler ancestor, for further experiments in the crime fiction field.

In *The Second Shot*, ABC cited Austin Freeman's Dr Thorndyke stories and A.E.W. Mason's *At the Villa Rose* in support of his contention that it was possible to retain reader interest in a crime once the culprit's identity had been disclosed.[2] Marie Belloc Lowndes had pioneered fictional exploration of the workings of the criminal or victim mind in *The Lodger* and *The Chink in the Armour*. In the Francis Iles novels, notes Julian Symons, "the reader knows what is being planned, and there is no question to be answered on the last page—yet tension and excitement are wonderfully maintained."[3] As Iles, observes Melvyn Barnes, ABC showed "with stunning panache, that there are countless ways of shocking the reader while completely eliminating the 'whodunit' element."[4] The books are models of their kind and milestones in the history of the detective story; their continuing attraction rests in "the interplay of character, the gaps between plot and execution, and in the air of suburban or small town normality with which Iles invests the whole thing."[5] The high quality of the writing compounds their appeal, most notably the author's often savage dissection of his characters' idiosyncrasies and his skillful delineation of their emotional osmosis. There is an added dimension—an ironic compassion. Where his predecessors, like Lowndes, had tended to deal with murder in the "old, accepted terms of abnormality . . . the Iles studies invariably point to the killer and say 'There but for the grace of God go I.'"[6]

Both *Malice Aforethought* and *Before the Fact* were regarded as startlingly innovative in their time, and they established a distinctive new subgenre of "inverted" novels, practitioners of which have ranged from Richard Hull, Henry Wade and Anthony Rolls to Margaret Millar, Andrew Garve and Ruth Rendell. Howard Haycraft notes that the ABC/Iles example also fostered an increased emphasis on characterization amongst writers of the more orthodox *roman policier*.[7] Publisher Victor Gollancz shrewdly publicized *Malice Aforethought* by leaking word that the unknown Francis Iles was in fact a very well-known writer, and ABC thoroughly enjoyed the resultant speculation about Iles's true identity. Johns calls it one of the great literary debates of the century.[8] E.M. Forster, Somerset Maugham, H.G. Wells, Warwick Deeping, Hugh Walpole, Eden Phillpotts, Aldous Huxley, even Osbert Sitwell, were some of the names put forward. Naomi Royde-Smith, of *Time and Tide*, was convinced that *Malice Aforethought* could not have been written by a woman; she pointed to the "excoriating portrayal of the young sensual women, either frankly amorous or evasive on sentiment, who are the true causes of Dr Bickleigh's crime" as evidence of Iles's intense disillusionment with females (and humanity in general). Other reviewers and readers were less sure, and put their money on Stella Benson, Rose Macauley or (unsurprisingly) Mrs Belloc Lowndes. There was also strong sentiment in favor of E.M. Delafield. It was not until September 1932 that an anonymous contributor to the *Irish Independent* linked Iles to ABC, partly by virtue of his apparent familiarity with the Devon countryside. A number of other critics, most notably the American man-of-letters Alexander Woollcott, suggested that Iles may be a collaboration between ABC and Delafield, or that Delafield might have been called in to improve ABC's rough drafts![9] (In the dedication to *As for the Woman*, ABC/Iles addressed his good friend Delafield: "A mean-minded young man, for a certain reason of his own, set on foot a rumour that you wrote my books for me, or at any rate had a hand in them. Alas, it is not so.")[10] *O England*'s title page officially indicated that A.B. Cox was also known as Francis Iles although ABC persisted in refusing to confirm the Iles/Berkeley linkage for several more years. No doubt he relished the creative leeway he had so long as his two crime-writing *personae* were kept separate. James Agate maintained that the relationship was an open secret by the time he reviewed *Jumping Jenny* in 1933 and, by the end of the decade, Haycraft observed that London and New York publishing circles no longer admitted any doubt that Cox, Berkeley and Iles were one and the same.[11] In the 1950s, ABC acknowledged (a little ruefully) that "there is now no secret about my being 'Francis Iles.' To regain a decent anonymity, I shall have to think about a new pseudonym."[12]

There are three Iles novels: *Malice Aforethought* and *Before the Fact* (both of them widely lauded as masterpieces), and the less successful but still interesting *As for the Woman*. ABC/Iles also published three criminous short stories (like the novels, "penetrating psychological studies of murder and horror told from the inside out").[13] In addition, the Iles byline was attached to the author's many book reviews and his nonfiction essays about the Rattenbury and Crippen murder cases (see chapter 7), a handful of A.B. Cox–style satires, and a straight romantic short story, "Sense of Humour" (again more in the A.B. Cox mold). There are also a number of distinctively Ilesian stage and radio play scripts and short story drafts in the ABC archive.

Malice Aforethought

In "My Detective Story," the *Punch* sketch in which he first hinted at his crime-writing ambitions, ABC stressed the importance of leading off with a "pithy, arresting and novel" opening paragraph: "it must leave a question in the mind of the reader so engrossing that he is willing to go to any lengths to find the answer."[14] The beginning of *Malice Aforethought* is a stunning example of this. (It also bespeaks its creator's determination to depart radically from Golden Age orthodoxy.) "It was not until several weeks after he had decided to murder his wife that Dr Bickleigh took any active steps in the matter. Murder is a serious business. The slightest slip may be disastrous. Dr Bickleigh had no intention of risking disaster."[15]

Dr Bickleigh is another in the procession of insignificant and ineffectual little men who display unsuspected capacities under stress in ABC's novels. He is much less likeable than Priestley, Chitterwick, John Sewell, Todhunter, or even Cyril Pinkerton (Panek dubs him a downtrodden "little twirp"), yet the reader cannot help sharing his anxieties and humiliations, and even feel a degree of sympathy for the predicaments he finds himself in.[16] Under-size, inarticulate, haunted by an unprepossessing provincial upbringing and mediocre education, constantly belittled by his gaunt and disapproving wife, Julia, Bickleigh is plagued by feelings of inadequacy. "In these days of glib reference to complexes, repressions, and fixations on every layman's lips, it is not to be supposed that Dr Bickleigh did not know what was the matter with him. He could diagnose an inferiority complex, and a pronounced one at that, as well as anyone else. But to diagnose is not to cure."[17] Acutely uncomfortable with the opposite sex, he compensates paradoxically by flirting with any passably attractive woman he meets, and he actually indulges in a joyless affair with a local girl. Disaster strikes when he becomes smitten with a neurotic young heiress, Madeleine Cranmere, who encourages his attention while simultaneously two-timing him. When Julia refuses to even consider granting him a divorce, Bickleigh cunningly plans her demise (by morphia) in the belief he will thus be free to marry Madeleine. Ironically, he administers the final lethal overdose on the very day he learns the calculating Madeleine is engaged to someone else.

An inquest rules Julia Bickleigh's death an accident, and the doctor smugly assumes he has committed a perfect crime. Inevitably however, village gossips begin to speculate that Julia may have been the victim of arsenic poisoning; Chatford, the husband of a young woman Bickleigh had "despoiled" earlier in the book, takes his suspicions to Scotland Yard. By this time, the doctor has grown so enamored of his own cleverness that he has begun to lose touch with reality. Vowing revenge on both Chatford and the duplicitous Madeleine and her new husband, he invites them all to tea, and plies them with potted meat sandwiches (he has infected the meat with a home-grown culture of botulism). Madeleine is only mildly ill, but Chatford is reported to be near death. Sublimely self-confident, and oblivious to the mounting suspicion around him, Bickleigh seeks to ensure his handiwork by visiting the ailing Chatford and reinfecting him. By doing so, he plays directly into Scotland Yard's hands; it turns out that the police had been investigating Julia Bickleigh's death for some time, and had enlisted Madeleine and Chatford to help flush the culprit out. Bickleigh is tried for his wife's murder and acquitted. In a glorious finale he is rearrested, and found guilty of killing Madeleine's husband. He goes to the gallows protesting his innocence. In fact, the alleged victim had died naturally (of typhoid); Bickleigh is ironically convicted by his own (typically) botched attempts to cultivate the botulism bacillus.

Like the other Iles novels, *Malice Aforethought* was clearly inspired by a real-life murder sensation (although the author later tended to deny it).[18] Major Herbert Rowse Armstrong, a solicitor in Wales, was hanged in 1922 for the murder of his domineering wife. He would probably have evaded detection had he not made a number of bizarre attempts on the life of a business rival, Oswald Martin. As well as mailing the unfortunate Martin a box of poisoned chocolates, Armstrong entertained his victim at tea with arsenic-laced scones. Martin was subsequently compelled to fend off a barrage of dinner and lunch invitations before the police finally arrested the homicidal major. Mrs Armstrong's arsenic-laden body was exhumed during the investigation. (ABC/Iles possibly also had the Crippen case in mind when he was planning the book.)

Malice Aforethought was originally published as a paperback, under the Mundanus imprint, by Victor Gollancz in 1931. In August–September of the same year it was serialized (with the subtitle *A Murder without a Mystery*) in the *Daily Express*. Critical response was overwhelmingly positive. The *Times Literary Supplement*, for example, applauded the triumphantly stage-managed conclusion; The *New York Times* dubbed the book "a fine psychological study of a distorted mind" and recommended it to "all who require substance in their mystery stories"; H.C. Harwood of the *Saturday Review* praised its "cynical humor, acute criminology, plausible detail and rapid movement." ("It makes you hug yourself with pleasure, unless you are one of those who think crime not quite nice.") The *English Review* called the novel "possibly the best shocker ever written. It is psychologically extraordinarily good."[19] Latter-day appraisals tend to be a little more qualified. Shibuk, for instance, argues that the first half of the book gives us ABC at top form but that the book deteriorates, "from high comedy to farce," once Bickleigh decides to commit a second murder; Strickland criticizes what he sees as a weakness in dramatic development in the plot.[20] By contrast, Symons calls the book "outstandingly original," and a landmark. ("If there is one book more than another that may be regarded as a begetter of the post-war realistic crime novel, it is this one.")[21] Art Bourgeau, in a five-star rating, maintains that the lead characters—"a selfish fool, a harsh harridan and a nymphomaniac bitch"—all get just what they deserve.[22]

In my view, this devastatingly ingenious novel ranks alongside *The Poisoned Chocolates Case* as ABC's finest work. It is populated with characters so uniformly unsympathetic that the reader can be excused for hoping that the ultimately pathetic doctor will triumph. I disagree with Strickland's insistence that, as a "womaniser, a hypocrite, and a vacillating, dithering sort of fellow," Bickleigh lacks the ability to command reader involvement.[23] The murderous little doctor is one of ABC's most fully developed characters. According to Julian Symons, "One achievement of the book is to make Bickleigh likeable, so that it is easy to see why the women of the community pity him, and the men say that he is a good little chap."[24] Desperate to escape his drab, brow-beaten existence, he deludes himself into believing that his wife's death does not amount to murder at all. ("His case was unique . . . Julia was impossible; life with Julia any longer was impossible; divorce by consent was impossible . . . only one course was inevitable. It was quite simple.")[25] Bickleigh excuses his subsequent attempts at homicide as divinely justified revenge. Of course, his fantasies have no basis; his clumsy failure to manufacture and infect his guests with the botulism culture accentuates his overall inadequacy, and the trial proves him more insignificant, ineffectual and incompetent than ever. *Malice Aforethought*'s other strengths include ABC/Iles's effective evocation of the limited and claustrophobic rural setting (Wyvern's Cross), his scathing portraits of Julia Bickleigh and Madeleine Cranmere, and his wittily satiric descriptions of courtroom procedure. The novelist's sense of humor is well in evidence throughout; justice might be served at the end but Bickleigh is condemned for a crime he did not commit. (The plodding Superintendent Allhayes is another of ABC's "mistaken detectives.")[26] The book was adapted as a BBC television serial in 1979, and featured an effective performance by Hywel Bennett as Dr Bickleigh.

Before the Fact

Where *Malice Aforethought* is an in-depth study of the mind of a murderer, *Before the Fact* goes one step further and tells its story from the point of view of the victim. Although the device was not entirely new (Mrs Lowndes's *The Chink in the Armour* predated it for instance), thanks to the writer's unquestionable skill the book enjoyed immediate and substantial success, and exercised an abiding long-term impact on his peers. (H.R.F. Keating judges it "one of the key texts in the history of crime fiction.")[27] It was originally published in the *Daily Express* (April–June 1932), under the more blatant title *Married to a Murderer*. Gollancz released it in book form shortly before the serial concluded. Like its predecessor, it reveled in a startling opening paragraph: "Some women give birth to murderers, some go to bed with them, and some marry them. Lina Aysgarth had lived with her husband for nearly eight years before she realized that she was married to a murderer."[28]

Johnnie Aysgarth, the outwardly charming, inwardly homicidal, villain of *Before the Fact*, is based on the notorious mass-poisoner William Palmer. A seemingly benign and genial man, Palmer is believed to have dispatched at least a dozen people using various poisons (he had a preference for strychnine and prussic acid). Several of his illegitimate children and other relatives were among his victims; he also systematically eliminated a number of creditors who were clamoring for him to settle his massive racing debts. Palmer's lesser crimes included forgery, embezzlement and theft (while still a teenager, he was dismissed from his first job for stealing money from letters). His wife, Annie, the daughter of an officer in the Indian army, brought a sizeable dowry to the marriage; her convenient death ultimately enabled him to collect on her life insurance. Other heavily insured victims were his brother, and an uncle who expired after a suspicious brandy-swilling contest. Justice finally caught up with Palmer in

1855, and he was executed at Stafford. ABC/Iles duplicates key aspects of his life and crime career in *Before the Fact;* Palmer's uncle becomes Beaky Thwaite in the novel, and Annie Palmer becomes Lina Aysgarth.

Lina (nee McLaidlaw) is a clever, no-nonsense young woman, acutely bored by the rural-middle-class milieu she inhabits, and cynically convinced that looks (not intelligence) are the only thing worth having for a woman. She has resigned herself to spinster-hood when she falls prey to the attractive Aysgarth. They marry and, little by little, she becomes aware that his likability masks a frightening unscrupulousness. Johnnie borrows 1,000 pounds for the honeymoon and rent on an impressive house, then admits he is unable to pay the money back. He proves to be a compulsive gambler; furniture is sold to provide betting wherewithal, a guest's valuable diamond pendant turns up in his pocket; he is sacked from his job for embezzling funds. Lina learns that he has been forging her signature, and she even fears he may have helped precipitate her ailing father's death; however, she leaves him only after she finds out he has been two-timing her with a housemaid and her best friend.

Lina attempts to start a new life in London and becomes romantically involved with a steady young artist who is keen to marry her. Yet she remains completely besotted by her good-for-nothing husband and cannot resist his pledge to mend his ways if she comes back to him. Johnnie really does seem to reform for a while, but he eventually slips back into his old ways and becomes increasingly desperate for money to cover his gambling debts. Lina's intuition warns her that he is planning to induce the death of his old friend and business partner, Beaky Thwaite. When Beaky does die, she believes herself as guilty as Johnnie ("Guiltier, because she was the responsible one of the two"). In the end, Lina realizes that she is destined to be her husband's next victim so he can claim her life insurance, but rather than forestall him or escape, she passively accepts her fate. The novel closes with her accepting a glass of milk from her uncharacteristically reluctant spouse. (We assume the milk is poisoned.)

One contemporary reviewer opined: "For sheer, nightmarish horror it has seldom been surpassed. . . . *Before the Fact* is remark-ably well done; it induces such a there-but-for-the-grace-of-God sensation that one remains shivering for hours." The *New States-man and Nation* observed: "Mr Iles is out to make us curdle. We curdled. This story of a dull woman who marries a man with charm and nothing else—no income, no honour, no decency, no kindness, no intelligence, only low cunning—is a dreadfully fasci-nating affair. The picture of apprehension, when the wife knows her charmer has decided to kill her, is scarcely tolerable." Else-where, the book was compared favorably to Henry James's *Turn of the Screw*; the *Times Literary Supplement* praised Iles's writing skill and the detachment which rendered the chain of events and characters plausible.[29] Two generations of critics and readers have tended to reinforce such plaudits: Howard Haycraft has called *Before the Fact* "unique and beyond price"; H.R.F. Keating dubs it "a masterpiece of (often savage) wit." Charles Shibuk calls it a contender for "the all-time honours list."[30]

For many critics (notably Shibuk, Haycraft, Steinbrenner and Penzler) the novel was an advance over even *Malice Aforethought*, and can be said to represent the pinnacle of ABC's achievement—in any of his literary incarnations. However, Panek, Strickland and Symons are all less wholehearted in their estimates. Panek judges the maddeningly passive Lina to be so insecure and men-tally limited that "any reasonable reader who experiences *Before the Fact* wants to strangle her for her abysmal stupidity even before she is murdered at the end of the book." Strickland con-cedes that the book is ABC's most successful "inverted" effort, but finds Lina's failure to avoid her own impending murder silly and difficult to believe in. (Even so, he acknowledges the character's ability to engage the feelings of the reader.)[31] Certainly the way in which Lina goes to her death like a lamb to the slaughter, solely because she is still so irrationally in love with her husband that she would rather die than face life without him, rather strains credibility. The book also tends to prolong the agony a little too much in places; the story dips after Lina leaves Johnnie, and the description of her romance with Ronald becomes tedious (at least Johnnie is not a bore). In my view, *Malice Aforethought* remains the more consistently diverting of the two books, and stands up better on rereading. (Symons, a devotee of the first Iles novel, believes its successor lacked sufficient elements of surprise. "Johnnie's behaviour is so wholly villainous throughout that it is difficult to believe he would not have been sent to prison.")[32] Interestingly, Shibuk tells us that the enigmatic ABC himself ultimately judged *Before the Fact* less than a success; his own toughest critic, he felt he had not been able to render Lina's character and motivation with sufficient clarity to satisfy his own standards.[33] On the credit side, the book contains a marvelous analysis of the rural social boundaries in interwar Britain ("For one who takes pleasure in despising his neighbors more than himself, the English countryside of this decade offers exceptional opportunities") and a blistering approach to questions of marriage and sexuality (ABC/Iles observes caustically: "She [Lina] had never realised that the percentage of happy marriages among the population of Great Britain is something under .0001").[34] There are also telling digs at the literary snobs who despise detective stories. "I love a good detective story," declares the intelligent Lina. (Johnnie, perhaps ominously, reads nothing else!) *Before the Fact* contains a witty, though rather affectionate, caricature of Dorothy L. Sayers in the successful crime novelist Isobel Sedbusk. "Not nearly as formidable as she looks," Isobel boasts of weighing 15 stone, "booms in proportion," sports black sombreros and masculine clothes, is an ardent feminist, and talks incessantly about murder (her stock-in-trade). It is Isobel who inadvertently provides Johnnie with the readily available (and undetectable) means to dispose of Lina.

Before the Fact achieved a kind of immortality when Alfred Hitchcock filmed it in 1941, under the title *Suspicion*. Surprisingly for Hitchcock, the film remained reasonably faithful to the book, allowing for compressions of time. Joan Fontaine is perhaps too physically attractive as Lina, but she is exceptionally effective in rendering the heroine's growing disquiet, while Cary Grant is a believable Johnnie. However, the film is vitally damaged by its ending, in which Johnnie turns out to have been innocent all along! (Reportedly, the film's original conclusion was faithful to the novel, but Hitchcock was forced to rework it because of fears that playing a killer would tarnish the dapper Grant's public image.)[35] The novel was republished in a revised edition in 1958; notwithstanding the author's dissatisfaction with the original though, he confined any changes to simply updating topical references. (C.B. Cochran was superseded by Cecil B. DeMille, H.G.

Wells by Somerset Maugham, Free Trade by politics; Gilbert Frankau and Michael Arlen gave way to Nevil Shute and Graham Greene, and mention was made of the end of World War II.)[36]

As for the Woman

Many of the original readers of the Iles novels would have been surprised at the author's unusual frankness in writing about human relations, particularly sexuality. Symons describes the books as "gamey," "rather like middle James in their fascinated hintings about sex."[37] At a time when the average detective story scarcely mentioned the physical aspects of love and marriage, ABC/Iles depicted Johnnie Aysgarth inflicting "terrifyingly improper things" on Lina, and berating her for being "a stingy bitch in bed."[38] Some found this taboo-breaking maturity rather too confronting; a *New York Times* reviewer, for instance, took exception to Dr Bickleigh's womanizing, insisting that one extra-marital affair should have been enough! Nor were readers always comfortable with other disturbingly anarchic undercurrents in the novels. Indeed, Symons once suggested that ABC himself may have been disconcerted by some of the extremely unorthodox ideas he set loose in the Iles canon: "There is a streak of feeling running through them that, without being exactly sadistic, shows a sort of cold-blooded enjoyment of both Dr Bickleigh's and Johnnie Aysgarth's activities."[39] ABC once confided to fellow writer Edmund Crispin that Victor Gollancz refused to publish the third and final Iles novel because he thought it "too sadistic."[40] While Crispin was never able to find the "slightest trace of sadism in it," it seems likely that Gollancz was alienated just as much by the book's eroticism and the complete absence in it of traditionally sympathetic characters. (J.D. Beresford of the *Manchester Guardian* judged it "frank to the point of indecency.")[41] *As for the Woman* (which was ultimately published by Jarrolds) is, in fact, a quite depressing work, peopled by unrelievedly drab or mediocre beings; it is essentially an extremely able (if not very likeable) character study which focuses on an uninspiring, almost "grubby," romantic triangle. It is a departure even from the other Iles books; the crime content is so decidedly secondary to the main theme of adultery that it seems likely ABC/Iles was intent on evolving into a straight novelist (albeit with a criminous slant) by this stage in his writing career. The book was announced as the first in a trilogy which would examine murder "as the natural outgrowth of character."[42]

As for the Woman was inspired by two celebrated murder trials, the Thompson-Bywaters and Rattenbury-Stoner cases. In both instances, a married woman's illicit relationship with an impressionable younger man resulted in the young lover's eliminating the husband. The novel's hero, Alan Littlewood, is based in part on Frederick Bywaters, the ship's steward who hanged for fatally stabbing Percy Thompson in 1922. Charged with incitement to murder, Edith Thompson was likewise executed, although probably more because of judge-and-jury outrage at her immorality then because of any real belief in her guilt. In a strikingly similar case a decade later, Alma Rattenbury and George Stoner were tried for battering to death Rattenbury's solicitor husband. Stoner was found guilty, but Mrs Rattenbury was acquitted, undoubtedly due to public concern that Edith Thompson had been executed unjustly. (ABC/Iles examined the Rattenbury case in considerable detail in the Detection Club anthology, *The Anatomy of Murder*. See chapter 7.) The fictional Evelyn Pawle—egotistical, neurotic, intellectually limited and self-centered—is a composite of both Mrs Thompson and Mrs Rattenbury, and her cuckolded spouse, Dr Fred Pawle, combines features of both murder victims. Unlike them, he survives and—as far as anyone in the book does—emerges the victor. ABC/Iles drew his title from the judge's summing-up in the Thompson case: "As for the woman, it may be that we can feel nothing but contempt for her." Evelyn reads a copy of the trial's transcript to her young lover in a key scene of the novel.

As for the Woman has a less complicated plot than its two predecessors. Alan Littlewood, an Oxford undergraduate and would-be poet, is the least promising member of an academically gifted family,[43] and suffers from a debilitating inferiority complex as a result. When he develops a patch on his lung, his mother arranges for him to convalesce with a G.P. in the coastal town of Seaport. Alan finds Dr Fred Pawle sarcastic and somewhat intimidating, but he is immediately attracted to the doctor's wife, Evelyn. He becomes more and more infatuated with the provocative older woman, breaks off his engagement to his unsophisticated young

fiancée, and with the doctor away overnight in London, he readily allows himself to be seduced. Blindly romantic, Alan deludes
himself into believing that the affair is "a unique love in its way
. . . for it had come into full flower in all innocence and purity, as a
kind of union of two sympathetic souls, long before the union of
their bodies had, as it were, merely put the final seal on it."[44] As
the affair progresses, he grows increasingly hostile towards Dr
Pawle.

The lovers spend a furtive night together in London, but—
unluckily—they are recognized there by a Seaport gossip. Fred
Pawle hears about the intrigue and confronts Alan, calling him a
fool to be taken in by the worthless Evelyn. Furious, Alan throws
a paperweight at his adversary, knocks him out, and is convinced
he has killed him. He is more than a little disillusioned by
Evelyn's selfish reaction; worried only for her own safety she
urges him to run away. He spends a miserable time on the run—
disguised as a woman, attacked by a dog, subjected to unwanted
advances—and he heads back to Seaport and telephones Evelyn.
He is stunned when Fred answers. It eventuates that Fred had
merely been knocked unconscious during the fight, and had
exacted his revenge by insisting that Evelyn send the young man
away dressed in women's clothing. Any lingering illusions Alan
might have about their "great love" disappear at a last meeting
with the flighty Evelyn in a dingy cafe. Significantly though, he
does not learn from the experience; the book's coda finds him
regaling his Oxford friends with a heavily revised version of the
story.

The chief strengths of *As for the Woman* are the author's skillfully constructed, multidimensional characters, particularly
Evelyn. Like Edith Thompson and Alma Rattenbury, Mrs Pawle is
not "a deliberately wicked woman. She had not and never had the
smallest intention of inflaming Alan against Fred more than was
necessary to make herself properly interesting to her young lover;
and even that was no more than instinctive. The last thing she
wanted to do was cause a breach between them."[45] In this regard,
the *New York Times* reckoned the book "a decided advance on its
author's earlier work," while other reviewers lauded Iles's "crisp,
clear expose of the flatness of late adolescence" and his skilled
description of Alan's family. Otherwise however, it was generally

agreed that the novel failed to come up to expectations. The concluding chapters (in which Alan is disguised as a woman) were deemed unconvincing and out-of-synch with the rest of the plot, while Sean O'Faolain suggested that, even for satire, Alan was "too roughly treated" and rendered "too idiotic." ("It is a grand book to read on the pier listening to the band or am I being just too awfully highbrow?") *As for the Woman* might be of interest as an introduction to Iles's work, argued another critic, but "as a development of his peculiar gift it has no exceptional merit."[46] More recent assessments tend to endorse this view; Charles Shibuk alone has observed: "Although it was far from being a total success, *As for the Woman* is one of Cox's most powerful and unjustly forgotten works." Shibuk believes that the frankly erotic novel was ahead of its time, and would probably have enjoyed much more popular and critical success had it been published a decade or so later.[47]

The combination of lukewarm reviews, poor sales and World War II paper shortages, undoubtedly dampened ABC's enthusiasm for any follow-ups to *As for the Woman*. One possible successor, called *On His Deliverance*, was announced for Jarrolds' spring 1939 list. Reportedly concerned with "the injustice in the jury system when the life of a man, accused of murdering his wife, rests on the word of a single unstrung, neurotic witness," the book never appeared (and no longer seems to exist). Nor did a second novel, a sequel to *As for the Woman*, in which Alan Littlewood gets married "to the wrong woman." Announced by Jarrolds in 1941, the book (known only as "a new novel") was apparently a study of "a completely amoral woman—not necessarily immoral though that usually follows." (Symons cites a rumor that the novel was unpublishable because of the frankness of its content.)[48]

Other Works by Francis Iles

The first of three excellent short crime stories by Iles was "Dark Journey," published in 1934. Ellery Queen has called it "a superb psychological study of crime and punishment."[49] In a plot which recalls Dreiser's *An American Tragedy*, an ambitious young solicitor's clerk named Cayley hopes to wed the boss's daughter and rise to a partnership in the firm. He is hindered by a regretted liaison with a working-class girl, Rose. With Rose determined to keep him, Cayley can think of only one way out. In the first sentence, ABC/Iles tells us "Cayley was going to commit murder"; he shoots her in the belief that his troubles will be over with her gone. The author describes Cayley's disbelief and remorse once he realizes just what he has done; in panic, he puts the girl's body in the sidecar of his motorbike, intending to dump it in a nearby quarry. However, the bike's engine continually stalls. He is confronted by a genial local policeman who demands to look at the "sack of potatoes" in the sidecar; Cayley shoots at him and escapes, only to crash through the protective fence above the quarry and plummet to his death. Ironically, the policeman remains unaware that Cayley had shot at him, and laughingly assumes that the young man inadvertently trod on the self-starter, causing the bike to run away with him!

"Outside the Law" (1934) is an unrelenting account of the last hours spent by an underworld trio under siege by the police. Smith, the leader, has coldbloodedly killed a policeman during a bungled robbery. He and his cohort, Pat, are sadistic thugs who enjoy killing and even revel in the final shoot-out. Their companion is a luckless, terrified immigrant, Muller, whom the pair had picked up half-starved off the London streets. Muller is a tragic victim of circumstances, horrified by his plight and revolted by his companions; when Pat and Smith turn on him and demand his gun, he refuses to give it up and ends up killing them in the desperate hope he will be able to placate the law. ("His brain, numbed by terror, had hardly registered the fact that he had killed two men. All he knew was that he was free . . . at last: free from Smith, free from the police.") At the story's chilling conclusion, Muller rushes out to surrender but is shot down by the law.[50]

"It Takes Two to Make a Hero" (1943) is somewhat lighter than its predecessors, and purports to be an anecdote told to the writer by a stranger at the Dodo Club. A young subaltern called Smith finds himself at a loose end while on leave in Brighton. Leafing through the local paper, he is intrigued by an advertisement, "Young lady has sporting prints for sale," and he foolishly decides to investigate. He finds the address, but a girl's voice tells him to come back later. When he returns he finds her dead (with her throat cut). Smith is terrified suspicion might fall on him and also uneasy how to explain why he was at the scene of the crime. He escapes up to London where his fiancée calls him a coward for not going to the police with his story, and subsequently breaks off their engagement. As it happens, the dead girl's killer is caught and all Smith's agonizing has been in vain. The Ilesian twist comes when the cowardly Smith turns out to be the Dodo Club's "one and only V.C. [Victoria Cross]."

The otherwise effective "It Takes Two to Make a Hero" is marred by a couple of quite unnecessary anti-Semitic references. (A repellent shopkeeper is described as a repulsive, frog-like old Jew.) When the story was reprinted in the more sensitive 1950s, its title was changed to "The Coward" and the anti-Jewish references mercifully deleted.[51]

A fourth Francis Iles story is such in name only. "Sense of Humour" is a pleasant but unexceptional little romantic comedy, the outcome of which hinges on a typically Coxian misunderstanding. Robert Fenton is intent on wooing and winning his childhood sweetheart, Marcia, a young widow living in out-of-the-way rural seclusion. Marcia refuses him point blank because she fears he has no sense of humor. However, Robert has allies among the villagers—he is disconcerted to learn that they are placing bets on a successful outcome for his suit. His car develops engine trouble, which means he cannot leave the village, and Marcia finds herself inundated with offers of free milk, butter and eggs provided the wedding takes place within six months. Marcia is convinced Robert has paid the villagers to do his wooing for him; she accepts this as proof that he does have a sense of humor and relents. (Robert, wisely, does not enlighten her.)[52]

ABC adapted both "Outside the Law" and "Dark Journey" for radio (the latter under the title "Checkmate"), and he composed a number of other radiologues which conform more to his Iles persona than to either A.B. Cox or Berkeley. "The House Opposite," for instance, details the thought processes of a woman who thinks she may have heard a murder being committed, and seen the "murderers" carry the "corpse" to a car. "Bus No. 36" was based on an unpublished Iles story, "A Little Black Hat"; it deals with theft and murder on the upper deck of a London bus. (The killer betrays himself by accidentally picking up his victim's hat instead of his own.) A three act stage play by Iles anticipates Joseph

Hayes' *The Desperate Hours;* "Hue and Cry" tells what happens when a fugitive from justice intrudes on the home of an ordinary family.[53]

As noted earlier, one of the earliest A.B. Cox short stories, "The Right to Kill" (1922), offered readers a foretaste of Iles. Dr Arbuthnot, a rural anesthetist, is present during a friend's appendectomy, and is horrified when the drugged patient starts to refer in intimate terms to his (Arbuthnot's) wife. Arbuthnot seriously considers eliminating his rival; he has no doubts as to his right to do so. "True, our paltry, emasculated laws did not recognize the punishment of death for his crime. Very well, he must be his own judge and his own executioner. Just a little too much chloroform . . . And no suspicion would ever rest on himself." A chance remark by the surgeon stops him at the last moment—fortunately, as his suspicions prove to be unfounded after all. The story's conclusion is trite and the execution immature, but the Iles touch is discernible.[54]

Johns identifies four more short stories, which were signed (or should have been) by Iles but were never published. "The Major was Right" is a light winemanship tale in the "Sense of Humour" vein. (It was rejected by the *Strand* in 1936.) In "The Benefit of the Doubt" an overworked young doctor finds nothing wrong with a patient he visits; the man dies a few hours later after taking medicine the doctor had prepared. From that time, the doctor is plagued by uncertainty: Was his original diagnosis wrong? Did he make a careless error in making up the medicine? Was the dead man's wife responsible? (She had remarried with unseemly haste.)

The lead character in "The Man Who Could Hear" is tormented by a voice which keeps saying "Three or four grains of arsenic"; it transpires that he is receiving telepathic messages from a doctor who is intent on the mercy-killing of his terminally ill wife. Another bitter tale, "It Isn't Fair," may well have resulted from ABC's court appearance in 1937. A man convicted of a minor motoring offense drives into an illegally parked car after he leaves the courthouse; the car belongs to the police constable who had been responsible for his court appearance. (We can speculate that this may have been wish-fulfillment on ABC's part.)[55]

In addition to his crime fiction, ABC/Iles joined a representative sampling of popular writers for two satirical anthologies,

Parody Party (1936) and *Press Gang* (1937), both edited by Leonard Russell. The former, dreamed up at a weekend house-party, consisted of parodies of well-known novels and novelists: E.C. Bentley tackled Dorothy L. Sayers (and *Gaudy Night*), J.B. Morton sent up John Buchan, L.A. Pavey Somerset Maugham, Rose Macauley Hemingway, and so on. The Iles contribution was "Close Season at Polchester," a clever parody of Hugh Walpole's Cornish Cathedral series. With a battle raging between Arch-Deacon Brandon and his rival, Canon Rounder, over Rounder's determination to buy a new trowel for the Close garden, the devil slips quietly into Polchester, disguised as a black cat. There are ominous warnings that a visiting stranger will be ritually killed by the local population—as per tradition. (The victim is selected because he is "a dreadful . . . sententious bore, and what can be worse than that? Whatever they may say about us here in Polchester, we're not bores.")

"Eastern Love Song" in *Press Gang* is a biting take-off of British courtroom procedures, and humorously satirizes the more ludicrous manifestations of 1930s censorship. The sketch purports to be the press report of a prosecution for obscenity; publishers Ding, Dong and Bell are charged with disseminating a book deemed pornographic because of its "unsavory" subject—"the gratification of sexual appetite." The 100-year-old judge holds his hands over his ears while the Attorney General reads selected passages from the book, which turns out to be an uncredited reprint of the Biblical *Song of Solomon*. By the end of the trial, it has joined the works of Shakespeare, Chaucer, Rabelais, Thomas Hardy, Dumas *fils* and Francis Iles(!) on the National Prudery League's condemned list.[56]

Another sketch "by Iles" was "The Lost Diary of Th*m*s A Ed*s*n," which appeared in the *Saturday Book 6* in 1946. A brief and rather tired piece of whimsy, it is a surreal catalogue of a famous (and extraordinarily creative) inventor's day-to-day achievements. Ed*s*n invents just about anything conceivable, including muffins, Leap Year, a machine for determining the sex of newts, the egg-whisk, a "new excuse for not going to Church," the BBC, a false nose, and the "super-mammoth extra-super-super hundred girl all singing all dancing centriplex teleprinter." The sketch is indistinguishable from ABC's contributions to *Punch* and

The Humorist twenty years earlier, and of negligible interest to the Iles enthusiast.

In the Francis Iles books, ABC radically redefined the Golden Age crime novel, as he explored the murkier depths of criminality, and focused on character, psychology and motivation at the expense of traditional puzzle ingredients. By the time of *As for the Woman*, the crime element had become a corollary to the author's preoccupation with his characters' interrelationships. Critics have judged the first two books, at least, as a major and decisive contribution to the genre, although ABC always remained ambivalent about his achievement. He once observed: "Crime fiction is for entertainment, and the attempt to make it significant is almost invariably a mistake; in the very rare cases where significance is achieved the result is a novel in its own right."[57] This comment, coupled with his adverse reaction when *As for the Woman* failed to elicit the critical raves that greeted its predecessors, suggests that ABC had a surprising lack of confidence in his own literary worth. *As for the Woman* was his last novel, and ABC gave up writing fiction altogether after the short story "It Takes Two to Make a Hero" (and the inconsequential sketch "The Lost Diary of Th*m*s a Ed*s*n") in the 1940s. Thereafter, apart from a handful of radio plays, he confined his activities to the criticism of crime fiction.

Quite fittingly, given that name's importance in the history of the genre, the book reviews bore the Francis Iles byline; it was Iles who kept ABC in the public eye up until his death, and Iles whom Julian Symons eulogized in an obituary article for the *Sunday Times*.[58] I look at the body of ABC/Iles literary criticism in the next chapter.

7

NONFICTION:
TRUE CRIME, BOOK REVIEWS AND POLITICS

Apart from the extensive body of fiction he produced in the 1920s and 1930s—sketches and satires, short stories and novels—and numerous unpublished stage and radio plays, ABC's output encompassed serious studies of real-life murder cases, literary criticism for several major newspapers, and a couple of passionately felt and expressed excursions into political and social comment.

True Crime

ABC's abiding interest in "the classical dramas of the central criminal court" (which he dubbed more absorbing than "any detective story ever written") is evident throughout his writing. "There is a complication of emotion, drama, psychology and adventure behind the most ordinary murder in real life, the possibilities of which for functional purposes the conventional detective story misses completely," he observed in the preface to *The Second Shot*.[1] Elsewhere he wrote: "Superior persons deprecate the interest in murder trials as morbid, or sensation-seeking . . . yet, if one faces the corollary, it is difficult to see how any normal person can remain indifferent to a trial such as this, and its result. One might go so far as to throw the challenge to the superior persons that actually it is the interest which is normal and indifference abnormal."[2] As a student of character, ABC was fascinated by the kind of minds which could envisage murder as a practical solution to their problems, and then translate that vision into action. ("I suppose, since most interests have an egotistical basis, as a psychological mechanic, if I may so describe myself to you, I am interested to compare these engines of the human chassis with my own, so like and yet, I sincerely hope, so unlike.")[3]

The Berkeley and Iles books are littered with references to classic crimes. In *The Poisoned Chocolates Case* for instance, the members of the Crime Circle draw parallels between their respective solutions to the puzzle (who killed Joan Bendix and why?) and several factual murder cases, on the assumption that "history repeats itself."[4] Thus Sheringham's conclusions draw on the Carlyle Harris case while his colleagues' solutions draw, in turn, on Molineux, Marie La Farge, Christina Edmunds, John Tawell and Dr Wilson. *Trial and Error* is based on the Pelizzioni and Mogni case. *Jumping Jenny*'s *mise en scene* is a macabre fancy-dress party where all the guests impersonate famous murderers and their victims: the Princes in the Tower, Madeleine Smith, Dr Crippen, Palmer the Poisoner, Mrs Pearcey, Mary Blandy, Jack the Ripper, Mrs Maybrick etc. (Significantly, the person generally assumed to be the killer comes dressed as "an undiscovered murderer," and the true culprit does not dress up at all.) In analyzing how publicity about a novel means of killing might stimulate a certain kind of mind to murder or suicide, Roger Sheringham compares *The Silk Stocking Murders* to those committed by Palmer, Dr Dove, Norman Thorne and Patrick Mahon.[5]

ABC obviously shared Sheringham's grudging admiration for the poisoner as "the criminal *par excellence*," conceitedly convinced that his/her murder can pass undetected.[6] At various times, his fictional victims are dispatched by nitrobenzine in chocolates, aconitine in pipe-tobacco, injections of curare, prussic acid in coffee or arsenic in medicine. The ABC Archive includes short, unpublished studies of four famous poisoners: George Henry Lamson, Franz Muller, William Palmer and Florence Maybrick.[7] Palmer provided the inspiration for the character of Johnnie Aysgarth in *Before the Fact*, and aspects of the Maybrick case served as the basis for *The Wychford Poisoning Case* and *Not to Be Taken*. *Malice Aforethought*'s Dr Bickleigh was created in the image of Herbert Rowse Armstrong, and *The Poisoned Chocolates Case* duplicated Armstrong's trick of anonymously mailing a lethal box of chocolates to an unsuspecting victim.

Another classic poisoner who excited the writer's interest was Crippen. In *Jumping Jenny*, the husband of the unlamented victim is described as "a charming man driven off balance by a terrible wife," just like the legendary doctor. "I've always felt sorry for

Crippen," remarks Sheringham in *The Wychford Poisoning Case*. "If ever a woman deserved murdering, Cora Crippen did."[8] ABC analyzed the case in a short essay, "Was Crippen a Murderer?" (by Francis Iles), in the collection *Great Unsolved Crimes*. Hawley Harvey Crippen was an American doctor, of rather dubious credentials, who settled in London with his shrewish, would-be actress wife at the turn of the century. He was tried and hanged for her murder in 1910.

A man of considerable charm and great kindness, Dr Crippen is remembered ironically as an "inhuman monster," whose name has become synonymous with murder. ABC/Iles argues that he was, in fact, the least certainly guilty of any of the so-called classical murderers. The psychology of the case is all wrong (the writer insists), "one does not remain gentle and kindly for 48 years and then reveal oneself as a fiend." Rather, ABC/Iles endorses Sir Edward Marshall Hall's theory that Cora Crippen's death was unintended, and that the doctor was, at most, guilty only of manslaughter. According to this viewpoint, Crippen dosed his wife with hyoscine in the belief she would be drugged long enough for him to enjoy a clandestine evening with his typist, Edith Le Neve. Inadvertently, he administered an overdose; he panicked, dismembered the corpse, buried it, and told all and sundry that his wife had returned to America (where she allegedly perished from pneumonia). He foolishly installed Miss Le Neve in his house and even paraded her at a charity ball in his late wife's jewelry. When the police became suspicious, the couple fled for Canada (Miss Le Neve disguised as a boy), but they were intercepted, thanks to the new invention of the wireless. ABC/Iles believes Crippen disadvantaged himself at the trial by lying in order to protect Miss Le Neve, and partly due to this chivalry; other analysts of the case (like Filson Young) have continued to view the doctor with considerable sympathy. A notable exception was the thriller-writer and criminologist William Le Queux, who once actually met Crippen, and later described him as "one of the most dangerous criminals of his century."[9]

Great Unsolved Crimes includes another ABC contribution, "Who killed Madame X?" (signed Anthony Berkeley). It speculates about the bludgeoning death in 1929 of a mysterious woman, Mrs Jackson, who (it turned out) had been a successful professional blackmailer. Her husband was charged with her murder, but the evidence against him was flimsy and he was acquitted. As ABC/Berkeley notes, the case (which was never solved) contained all the stock ingredients of the mystery story—shadowy victim with murky past, attack by an unknown assailant, anonymous threatening letters before the event, suspicion falling on the wrong person, disappearance of the weapon, and so on. ("Instead of fiction copying fact, fact here definitely copies fiction.") The writer deduces that the culprit must have been one of Mrs Jackson's former victims or a friend of one of her victims; in that case, he queries, "can we be altogether sorry that the case of Madame 'X' will now remain a mystery forever?"[10]

The Rattenbury case was reportedly ABC's favorite real-life crime;[11] he examined it in two essays, a lovingly detailed in-depth study ("The Rattenbury Case") in the Detection Club compilation *The Anatomy of Murder* (1936), and a brief article, "Mrs Rattenbury," in *The Strand*, May 1943.[12] Francis Rattenbury, a 63-year-old Bournemouth architect, was bludgeoned to death with a mallet in 1935; his much younger wife, Alma, and her 19-year-old lover, George Stoner, were charged with murder and tried together at London's Old Bailey.[13] Stoner was found guilty while Mrs Rattenbury was acquitted; she suicided three days later, and Stoner's sentence was subsequently commuted.

The case was simple, even trite, but ABC/Iles believed that the character of Mrs Rattenbury elevated it above its sordid circumstances: ". . . it is the foolish woman who must be blamed ultimately for most murders. Often she gets murdered herself, and usually she well deserves it. In other cases she is the incitement, often unconscious but none the less deadly . . . Outside fiction it is comparatively rare to find man murdering man for cold-blooded gain, as Palmer murdered Cook, or Lamson his nephew, without an unbalanced woman somewhere in the background to add a tinge of warmth to the affair."[14] Many aspects of the Rattenbury-Stoner case recalled the Thompson-Bywaters trial of 1922; both women were egocentric neurotics, wrapped-up in themselves, excitable, hysterical, able to impress the opposite sex. Neither thought of herself as in any way a bad woman, or living an immoral life. "A faculty for detached self-analysis is rare," observes ABC, "and quite a high degree of it is required before a woman can rise, scantily-clad, from a lover's lap, a glass in one hand and a cigarette in the other, and remark: 'Well, well, I suppose this is an orgy, and I am an improper person to be taking part in it.'"[15] The women's fondness for fantasy arguably spurred their susceptible young swains to homicide. Stoner was a rather less sympathetic being than the fundamentally decent Frederick Bywaters. According to ABC, he acted in the belief that a rich wife would be his for the taking once Francis Rattenbury was out of the way. It was widely believed that Edith Thompson had died unjustly, found guilty of adultery rather than murder, just as Florence Maybrick was convicted more by public outrage over her extramarital activities than any real proof she poisoned her husband. Undoubtedly (argued ABC), Alma Rattenbury was acquitted because Mrs Thompson was hanged, and her cause was assisted immeasurably by a judge determined not to be responsible for a repeat of the Thompson execution.[16]

In ABC/Iles's view, Alma Rattenbury was a much more sympathetic human being than she was portrayed in the popular press, and he decried the sensationalism which attended reports of the trial. Arguing that hounding by unscrupulous reporters probably "unhinged an already loosened mind" and pushed her to suicide, he predicted: "One day, perhaps, a reporter of the gutter-press, in a fit of decent feeling will murder the proprietor who gives him his orders, and then we shall have a trial worth hearing."[17] Other analysts of the case have shared ABC's opinion of the leading protagonist, notably F. Tennyson Jesse in the *Notable British Trials* series and Edgar Lustgarten in *The Woman in the Case* (1955).

Book Reviews

ABC was one of a number of Golden Age writers who turned their enjoyment of reading the latest mystery or thriller to good (and profitable) effect by penning regular book reviews. Dorothy L. Sayers was perhaps the most successful; she contributed literate and witty critiques of current crime releases in a weekly column for the *Sunday Times* from June 1933 to August 1935. Nicholas Blake, E.R. Punshon and F. Tennyson Jesse were engaged in similar capacities by *The Spectator, Manchester Guardian* and *Times Literary Supplement*, while across the Atlantic, Dashiell

Hammett wrote for the *Saturday Review* and *New York Evening Post.*

As Francis Iles, ABC contributed critiques to the *Daily Telegraph* (1933-36) and the magazines *Time and Tide* (1932-33) and *John O'London's Weekly* (1938), as well as monthly columns for the *Sunday Times* (1953-56) and the *Manchester Guardian* (1956-70).[18] While the 1930s reviews ranged over a broad spectrum of modern fiction (including the odd detective story), the later reviews focused specifically on crime fiction; ABC/Iles's contributions to the *Sunday Times* and *Guardian* remain of particular interest for the light they shed on his vision of the genre, and for his perceptive estimates of the work of his peers. After World War II, book reviews constituted the writer's sole published output.

Notwithstanding his own profound impact on the evolution of the detective story into the crime novel in the 1930s, ABC/Iles admitted to a strong affection for the "straightforward, honest-to-goodness puzzle," and he lamented that the classical whodunit was on the way to extinction in the 1950s.[19] As one who greatly preferred "the penny-plain type of crime story to the tuppence-coloured," he objected to being harrowed when he wanted to be entertained. ("Whether a criminal psychopath is a fit subject for a thriller is a matter of opinion," he wrote in a review of Robert Bloch's *Psycho*.)[20]

Among the traditional detective story's leading exponents, he had a particular fondness for Agatha Christie, whom he praised as a "diabolically ingenious illusionist," the "biggest shot" of the "classical sixth form." He judged even her lesser efforts (like *Dead Man's Folly* or *4.50 from Paddington*) superior to most other writers' best; in ABC's view, anyone who found Hercule Poirot boring must be determined not to enjoy him or herself. In the 1930s, he judged Dorothy L. Sayers "the most important of our detective writers" and her novels "what the detective story for sophisticated people should be." (He took exception, however, to the centrality of the love interest in Sayers's *Gaudy Night,* and expressed concern that "maternal affection" was in danger of turning Wimsey into "a stuffed prig.")[21] Other Golden Age practitioners he admired were Ngaio Marsh, Belton Cobb, Georgette Heyer, Henry Wade ("a born novelist, with a novelist's feeling for character, scenery—and the King's English"), John Rhode and Michael

Innes. Gladys Mitchell he found "somewhat uneven" (although Mrs Bradley was his "favourite crocodile"), and he judged Elizabeth Ferrars's plots "static." He failed to share the general regard for Margery Allingham, generally finding her books to be baffling rather than satisfying, and decrying her reliance on "wild improbabilities of human behaviour."[22] Of the younger generation of British writers, he admired Julian Symons, Colin Watson, Michael Gilbert, George Bellairs and Christianna Brand.

More often than not he was generous in reviewing newcomers to the genre; he accurately predicted great things for Ruth Rendell after *From Doon with Death*, for instance. P.D. James's *Unnatural Causes* was "told with unusual distinction." However, he was consistently critical of what he saw as a decline in writing standards. "Surely the publishers' offices contain *one* person who knows the difference between good and illiterate English?" he protested in response to the proliferation of "cheap jargon" and grammatical howlers in postwar crime novels. "Fancy James Bond not knowing that while pheasants are hung, human beings are hanged!" was one observation; in reviewing Michael Innes's *The New Sonia Wayward* in 1960, he declared himself shattered to find "an Oxford don and Shakespearean scholar using the American ignoramus word 'disinterest' to mean not 'impartiality,' for which there might be some excuse, but 'lack of interest,' for which there is none."[23] Elsewhere he suggested that some writers' fashionable propensity for describing the purely personal problems of their detectives tended to detract from the main interest of their novels. Similarly, he maintained that insufficient attention was often paid to stylistics like plausible denouements: "It is the ending which is the Achilles' heel of crime writing. So many otherwise good books are ruined by pandering to the convention which decrees a shock of some sort in the last few pages."[24]

ABC/Iles's likes and dislikes in the genre had a distinctly nationalist bias. He admitted to prejudice against over-lush writing, sentimentality, "and that kind of portentous pretentiousness met with chiefly in books from America, which seem to be trying to cram a quart into a pint-size thriller." At one point he wrote: "The Americans never seem to do things by halves . . . Quite nine-tenths of American thrillers, and even detective stories, fall slap into one of two categories: the tough or the sentimental . . . And when they are tough they are very, very tough, and when they are sentimental they are slushy." He had little patience with the hard-boiled school of Chandler, Hammett and Cain (he parodied it brilliantly in "The Policeman Only Taps Once"), and he disliked the character Ellery Queen intensely ("a pompous windbag who never uses five words when fifty will do"). *The Warning Bell* by Stephen Ransome, for instance, was reviewed as "completely professional, completely artificial, and completely American." M.G. Eberhart's plotlines were dubbed "nonsensical."[25] ABC/Iles was also highly critical of those transatlantic writers who set their books in England without undertaking the necessary research—resulting in such incongruities as American courtroom procedures transplanted into the Old Bailey. (Judges pounding the gavel, counsel snapping "objected to as immaterial and irrelevant . . . and all sorts of other Alice-in-Wonderland features.") Regarding Holly Roth's descriptions of the British bobby, he noted wryly that Scotland Yard men did not as a rule talk like dons, and "we practically never arrest anyone for murder on no evidence at all." ABC was generally nonplused by the U.S. legal process as depicted in fiction: "What an extraordinary legal system," he declared, "in which evidence seems to count for little and a conviction can hardly be obtained without a confession, which confession is promptly repudiated in court! Alice in Wonderland could hardly do it better." Amanda Cross seemed to have "some very odd ideas about the average English 'mystery.'"[26]

However, a select number of U.S. writers did manage to break through ABC's anti-American bias, and excite his admiration. He conceded that Erle Stanley Gardner was "a superb and prolific craftsman," and he had high praise for Patricia Wentworth, Emma Lathen, Patricia Highsmith (whose "ruthless inhumanity" compared favorably with "the sickly treacle and semi-hysteria with which so many American woman crime-novelists deluge their stories") and Margaret Millar (whom he judged to be "head and shoulders above most of her compatriots"). The new Rex Stout was "always an occasion for rejoicing," and Lilian Jackson Braun's cat-detective Koko was deemed "one of the best characters in crime fiction just now." Stanley Ellin's *Mystery Stories* was "as brilliant a collection of stories by a single author as has been published during the last 25 years," and Harry Kemelman's Rabbi

Small stories were recommended as "far better novels than most modern novels are." Evelyn Berckman's *She Asked for It*, which he reviewed in his final "Criminal Records" column in September 1970, was "a tour-de-force of tenseness and shivery horror."[27]

ABC/Iles's reviews were pithy, direct, often caustic and tinged with literary anglophilia (Denzil Batchelor's *The Taste of Blood* was lauded as "blessedly English," for example), but he was objective enough to be able to appreciate able storytelling and intelligent plotting on their own merits, and regardless of national origin.[28] Read today, when a large proportion of the books and authors listed have fallen into obscurity, the critiques highlight his extensive knowledge of the genre and, right up to the end of his life, his undampened enthusiasm for it.

An interesting footnote to ABC/Iles's career as literary critic was his involvement in a minor but deeply felt one-man crusade for improved standards of reviewing in the 1930s. On more than one occasion, he fell foul of writers who found his assessments of their labor insufficiently flattering, and he did not hesitate to defend the integrity and responsibility of his position. Indeed, he represented himself as something of a "a voice crying in the wilderness" (where back-patting by reviewers of their friends' and colleagues' work was all too common). "Alas, alas, harsh is the way of a reviewer, and thorny his path," he lamented after a friend cut him dead at their club because he had written something "nasty" about the man's latest opus. A letter of complaint from another offended writer prompted ABC to demand: "Is the critic . . . to be 'kind' or is he to take the firm line that such a square peg is not to be encouraged into any further attempts on such a round hole? . . . There would be no need of the question if kindness were not today so prevalent." Clearly (and increasingly), believed ABC, absolute standards of criticism were being abandoned in favor of reviewers' personal prejudices. ("Many a novel receives cruel and biting notice from some critic who belongs to some different clique from the author.")[29]

The climax of ABC's crusade was a joyfully tongue-in-cheek letter to *Time and Tide* which is worth reprising at some length here. The tone is comic—A.B. Cox, humorist, in full flight—but the underlying message (and the author's exasperation) glaringly clear:

Sir—I am much chagrined to learn from certain of your correspondents that it is the practice of authors to wine, dine, or make other delightful presents to reviewers, in order to obtain favourable reviews.

Sir, why is it that these *douceurs* never come my way? What is wrong with my technique that no author ever courts me with Chambertin 1923 or Golden Plovers or *foie gras* toast (no more than just *passed* through the oven, please)? Why, when I want so many quite inexpensive articles and have superlatives *ad lib* to dispense in exchange, have I never been approached in the usual way? . . . Why is it that, when . . . all other reviewers are bursting with the good things thrust upon them by hopeful authors, I, apparently alone, go wineless and dinnerless.

Sir, my case is even more pitiable still. Not only do authors refuse to dine and wine me: they even try to deprive me of free coffee. Only the other evening a lady novelist, of no small but at the same time no overwhelming reputation, cancelled her acceptance of an invitation to drink evening coffee in Bloomsbury on learning from her hostess that I was to be present. The reason, frankly and fearlessly given, was that out of all the tribe of reviewers I alone had ventured to criticise instead of merely praising, in the orthodox way, her last novel; and neither she nor her husband cared to meet such a low person. [ABC is advised that her reaction is] not inordinate vanity . . . but the natural disgust of one player of the game for another who breaks the rules. There is, in fact, something very wrong in my technique, which must be costing me goodness knows how many dinners and simply countless bottles of wine—perhaps even scarf-pins and motor cars. [Perhaps he should have] notified the lady in advance that my bribe for indiscriminate praise of her novel would be two bottles of champagne and one of anchovy sauce, or ought I to have praised blindly and then waited in confidence for what might arrive on my doorstep the next morning?

Francis Iles[30]

Politics

The Berkeley, Iles and A.B. Cox books and stories are set in the traditional Golden Age neverland of country house-parties, suburban drawing-rooms, Wodehousian London or rural villages, populated by the standard mix of 1920s hedonists, "bright young things" and "silly asses," imperious dowagers, shady plutocrats, stiff-upper-lip ex-servicemen, pallid heroes and salon intellectuals. For the most part it is an idealized middle-class England, cozy, insular and detached from the interwar realities of economic Depression, mass unemployment, social cleavage and political instability. The writers of detective stories and light fiction saw themselves primarily as entertainers; their work inevitably contained elements of satire or burlesque, but most of it tended to avoid more overt social comment. There were notable exceptions however. Dorothy L. Sayers's *The Unpleasantness at the Bellona Club*, for instance, underlines the problems of readjustment for shell-shocked Great War veterans in an indifferent Britain; *Gaudy Night* is, to some degree, an extended dissertation on the role of women in postwar society. Raymond Postgate's *Verdict of Twelve* contains a dramatic analysis of accelerating anti-Semitism (one almost unique in detective fiction of the period). While Roger Sheringham's early investigations take place on the familiar and limited turf of *The Family Witch* or *The Professor on Paws*, they frequently parody aspects of interwar culture or behavior, and from the early 1930s the Berkeley and Iles books contain illuminating references to topical socioeconomic and political questions. The rise of Fascism and Nazism, the Spanish Civil War and the critical state of international affairs figure prominently in conversations in *Trial and Error, Not to Be Taken* and *Death in the House*. Closer to home, *As for the Woman* contains sardonic and probing observations about oppressive social mores in English seaside towns and provincial cities: "semi-detached life in a semi-genteel road that was the middle class equivalent of a back street, with retired grocers leaning over your fence and forcing their inept conversation on you at the wrong moments." (Day-to-day existence in the town of Elmsford is described as typical of "the essential vulgarity of English town life.")[31] The otherwise irreverent *Top Storey Murder* features a disconcerting portrait of genteel poverty (mid-Depression) in a shabby London apartment building. In *Before the Fact*, crime novelist Isobel Sedbusk is "inclined to take the gloomy view of England's future; perhaps not more gloomy than the governors of England's present warranted." "Things are certainly in a bad way everywhere," acknowledges Lina Aysgarth, referring to the summer of 1932 when (as the author puts it) "England at last had to atone for the third-rate minds that had been governing her since the war by facing the fact that not even a nation can go on conveniently living above its income to keep a political party in office; and jobs were impossible to obtain."[32] *Death in the House* again targets what ABC saw as the ineptitude of British politicians and the culpable complacency of the Great British Public. The writer made a more concentrated attack on 1930s Britain in a full-length polemic.

Incensed at what he saw as the venality of professional politicians, and the proliferation of petty laws and regulations which unjustly inhibited the "ordinary citizen," ABC felt compelled to put his thoughts on paper. Indeed, he insisted that he had a duty as a citizen, taxpayer, humanitarian and honest man, to denounce oppression, injustice and roguery, be it at the seat of Government itself. *O England,* signed A.B. Cox (Francis Iles), was published by Hamish Hamilton in 1934. The title was drawn from Shakespeare's *Henry V*: "Oh England!—model to thy inward greatness, like little body with a mighty heart—what mightst thou do, that honour would thee do, were all thy children kind and natural."

ABC believed he represented the views of the proverbial "plain man," a large, voiceless section of the population. The longer the "typical ordinary citizen" lived in England, he argued, the more restive he became under the conditions of life being forced on him. He was treated as an irresponsible, almost imbecile, child by Government, granted little or no liberty in ordering his private life, forced to endure endless bureaucratic restrictions, compelled to watch those responsible for his welfare dillying and dallying with questions of vital importance and legislating on class lines. "A Government which puts bits into the mouths of all its citizens, and then tugs at the reins, is not a good Government," he averred.[33]

In ABC's view, the country had become a joke. "Great Britain is, without any doubt at all, by far the most civilised Major Power in the world . . . Then how is it that one hears people in Great Britain beginning to say: 'The country simply isn't worth living in any longer?'"[34] Outside the Fascist states, there was nowhere in the world in which personal liberty was so restricted. Such infringements of the majority desire as excessive taxation, antiquated divorce laws and early closing hours in hotels persisted simply because of self-seeking politicians and the public's laziness and apathy. He proposed a *Nova Charta* for rectifying the situation: a term of rest for politicians and the formation of a temporary National Government, made up of ordinary citizens from all classes, trades and professions, owing allegiance to no political creed or theory, and with a brief to clear up the mess, enact reforms and wipe out abuses and injustices. To that end, he recommended enlisting women: national and international affairs needed viewing "in the practical, unacademic way in which the female mind works . . . [with] none of the dreadful male respect for red tape."[35] In particular, he stressed the necessity for an education system which would enable more people to differentiate "gems from paste."

O England was a thought-provoking treatise which made a number of valid points. The *Times Literary Supplement* praised the author's "impetuous" defense of the "lesser liberties" of the citizen and his "sympathetic imagination" when discussing the plight of the "manual working classes." However, the book was blighted by careless inaccuracies about tax-rates, death duties and import levies, and ABC's demands that old prejudices be swept away could not disguise the conventionality of his own biases.[36] His patronizing, if well-intended, statements on women now seem particularly dated. (He contends that women are too easily influenced, guided by emotion rather than reason.) In retrospect, *O England* is an oddity, a product of its time, and of interest mainly for the insights it gives us into its creator's thinking. His most deeply felt piece of writing, it met with a distinctly lukewarm response from the reading public; an advertised follow-up called *You and I and All of Us* never materialized.

As I noted earlier, ABC compiled a book-length journal of his attempts to prevent the marriage of Edward VIII and Wallis Simpson, and thus invalidate the abdication. Like his critique of the British Government in *O England*, it was an issue close to his heart—but again, conviction did not make for readability. Johns calls the unpublished "Commoner and King: A Journal" "detailed but dull stuff," unpublishable then as now.[37] (The journal is referred to in Philip Ziegler's biography of Edward VIII.)[38]

8

CONCLUSION

When we consider that he produced the bulk of his literary output in the short period from 1922 to 1939, ABC can be seen as a remarkably prolific writer, and more versatile than has generally been supposed. His publications encompassed 21 novels, two book-length collections of sketches, numerous short stories, a couple of hundred miscellaneous skits, sketches and articles, a full-length political essay, radio and stage plays, two comic operas, criminological analyses and an extensive body of criticism. In addition, existing manuscripts and references to other unpublished titles testify to a tantalizingly extensive apocrypha. The unpublished novel "An Amateur Adventuress," the political journal "King and Commoner" and various short stories are extant, but we can only speculate on the whereabouts of such works as "Poison Pipe," "On His Deliverance" or "You and I and All of Us."

Yet the modern reader knows only a fraction of ABC's writing. The lack of recognition accorded the full range of his crime and mystery fiction seems particularly incongruous, given his undisputed importance in the history of the genre and the widespread resurgence of enthusiasm for detective stories in the decades since he died. Indeed, the overall quality of ABC's contributions to the form eloquently refutes Isobel Sedbusk's claim (in *Before the Fact*) that anyone can write a detective novel. ("Its just a matter of hard work, that's all.")[1] Critics have frequently focused on the significance and originality of *Malice Aforethought* and *Before the Fact*, or on the merits of *The Poisoned Chocolates Case*, but have often tended to overlook ABC's other finely crafted mysteries. Their current lack of availability is evidence of an unwarranted neglect.

LeRoy Panek and William Bradley Strickland have both speculated on the reasons for this neglect. Strickland suggests that the

113

books date badly because of their preoccupation with voguish interwar conceptions of psychology. Panek argues that ABC's prose style could be "elephantine, awkward and dull" on occasion, and that most of his stories followed the same basic plot pattern. Both critics agree that the Berkeley and Iles novels suffer from a lack of engaging and sympathetic characters: ABC's people are "either weak or vain or stupid, and this sort of person is hardly the sort that will survive in popular fiction," writes Panek.[2] By contrast, Melvyn Barnes lauds ABC's ability to enlist sympathy for the murderer Bickleigh in *Malice Aforethought*.[3] Certainly, the reader cannot but share the doctor's feelings when he wakes up in a fever of terror over the police's interest in his wife's demise. Similarly, we share Cayley's belated remorse in the short story "Dark Journey," and fully understand why the anguished Muller kills his underworld cohorts in "Outside the Law."

However, Panek concedes that what appear to be negative features of ABC's writing may well have been deliberate choices on his part. For instance, the essential similarity of the plots—particularly their emphasis on the multiple solution—echo the fact that reasoning by detectives in real life must be based on trial and error. Sheringham speaks for his creator when he criticizes the old-fashioned detective story for allowing only one deduction to be drawn from any one fact. (In reality, a hundred plausible inferences might be drawn from the same clue in real life.)[4] ABC's style of plotting (unraveling a puzzle or problem) is also gratifying for the reader. "Thus when Cox takes one set of facts and applies them equally to several people we get satisfaction and amusement beyond that which we would receive if one set of facts were applied to one person only."[5] Of course, ABC's persistent employment of the multiple solution plot was also an attack on the seriousness of the detective story. *The Poisoned Chocolates Case*, for instance, revels in eight solutions, not one of which would ever stand up in court. Not only do the Berkeley and Iles novels challenge detective story traditions; in lampooning the stuffy conventions of the genre, they stand them on their head. *Top Storey Murder*, as Panek has noted, makes news out of "dog bites man": the routine police answer, rather than Roger's "baroque concoction," proves to be the correct one.[6] The same is true of *The Vane Mystery*. In *The Wychford Poisoning Case* the murder turns out to be not so at all. Again, in *The Layton Court Mystery*, death is the result of self-defense rather than murder, and the culprit defies convention by being Watson to Sheringham's Holmes; *The Second Shot* is narrated by the killer (just as in Agatha Christie's celebrated *Murder of Roger Ackroyd*). *The Wintringham Mystery* revisits the hoary old cliché of "the butler did it." In *Malice Aforethought*, the killer gets his comeuppance—but he hangs for the wrong crime. In *Jumping Jenny* we seem to be privy to the culprit's identity and motivation from the time the murder is committed, while in *Trial and Error*, we have the murderer desperately fighting to convince the police of his guilt in order to save an innocent man.

The multiple solution is one of three major recurring themes and plot devices which distinguish the Berkeley and Iles novels and short stories from their run-of-the-mill contemporaries. All three are interrelated and are underscored by the writer's rebellion against the inflexible (and unrealistic) moral order depicted in the traditional detective story. Just as the multiple solution reflects reality, so does the figure of the fallible detective. Apart from the only intermittently successful Sheringham, ABC gives us the initially mistaken Stephen Munro in *The Wintringham Mystery/ Cicely Disappears*, the astute but misguided Allhayes in *Malice Aforethought*, the police in *Not to Be Taken*, and even the usually triumphant Mr Chitterwick in *Trial and Error*. The fallible sleuth represented a significant departure from the superhuman norm of its day.

Perhaps the most radical innovation made by ABC was his almost anarchic redefinition of murder as an offense against the moral order. This included a quite contentious revaluation of natural justice versus the legal process. As early as *The Layton Court Mystery*, the genial victim Stanworth turns out to be an unscrupulous blackmailer; thus the suspects are automatically rendered comparatively sympathetic, and Sheringham dismisses outright any suggestion that the likeable culprit complicate matters by involving the police. (Stanworth's death is passed off as suicide.) In subsequent books the victims are more often than not outstandingly unattractive individuals—for example, the hypochondriac Bentley, the adulterous Mesdames Vane, Bendix and Warrington, the caddish Eric Scott-Davies, the miserly victim of *Top Storey Murder*, the secretary with a shady past in *Murder in the*

Basement, the shrewish Julia Bickleigh, the unbalanced and vindictive Mrs Stratton, the oppressive Rose Fenton (in "Dark Journey"), the scheming butler in *The Wintringham Mystery,* the "poisonous bitch" Jean Norwood in *Trial and Error,* and the Machiavellian Mr Pidgeon in *Panic Party.* In *Mr Priestley's Problem,* the eponymous hero is glad to have rid the world of an extortionist. ("I've always considered shooting the only cure for blackmailers.") Among ABC's few sympathetic victims are the clergyman's daughter, Janet Manners, and her fellow victims in *The Silk Stocking Murders,* Mrs Bracey in "The Wrong Jar," Lina Aysgarth (notwithstanding that she seems to be either awe-inspiringly stupid or culpably masochistic) and John Waterhouse in *Not to Be Taken* (although Waterhouse dies by mistake). In general ABC's murder victims contrast unfavorably with such fundamentally decent and likeable culprits as the altruistic Lawrence Todhunter and the killers in *Not to Be Taken, Jumping Jenny, The Poisoned Chocolates Case, The Second Shot* and *Panic Party.*[7] Time and again, ABC's murderers escape the consequences of their actions; their victims are pre-eminently deserving of their fates, and the world is deemed all the better for their leaving it. In the Berkeley/Iles world murder can be justified on occasion, and he sees no reason why otherwise admirable human beings should pay exorbitantly for an action which has benefited humanity. "I believe in Murder," declaims Isobel Sedbusk in *Before the Fact,* "All sorts of people ought to be murdered. It's a great pity one isn't allowed to do it."[8] In two thirds of the novels, the killer is never made to account for his/her crime; thus natural justice can be seen to triumph over the shortsighted demands of (British) law.

"If Cox came to stand for anything in the Golden Age, he came to stand for psychology," writes Panek.[9] Fascination with the vagaries of human behavior preoccupied both the writer and his fictional alter egos and accounted for his ongoing enthusiasm for true crime cases and his bids to transcend the crime puzzle-story in his criminous character studies. As Francis Iles, he surmounted the detective story's obsession with physical clues; he replaced them with psychological clues and focused his main attention on the criminal rather than on the sleuth. In the process, suspense was substituted for the adventure ingredient.[10] *Malice Aforethought* dissects the mind of a murderer, *As for the Woman* the mind of a would-be killer, and *Before the Fact* the mind of a victim. (In the Iles books, ABC "wields a juvenalian lash which cuts again and again into the nasty perversity of human behaviour.")[11]

Strickland has observed that the Berkeley and Iles writing personae illustrate the parallel development of two major branches of the English crime story, the intricate Agatha Christie–style puzzle, and the psychologically realistic novel now associated with such practitioners as Julian Symons or Ruth Rendell. In reality, the differences between the two personae were more apparent than real at times.[12] *Trial and Error*, for example, now seems much closer in style to Iles than to the Sheringham books, yet it boasts a distinctively Berkeleyesque multiple-solution plot, a devastating surprise finish, the presence of Mr Chitterwick and the recurring motif of the mistaken detective. The body of his work can be seen as transitional in the genre, "a compromise between social comedy and satire on the one hand and psychological realism on the other."[13] Accordingly, elements of the writer's other persona, the humorist A.B. Cox, are well in evidence throughout the mystery novels.

Anthony Berkeley Cox commenced his writing career as a humorist and satirist, author of comic novels, light operas and scores of skits and sketches published under his own name. He made his reputation, and found fame and fortune, as Anthony Berkeley, an ingenious writer of urbane and skillful detective stories in the traditional puzzle mold, and as Francis Iles, innovator of the crime novel as character study. In his two criminous guises (to paraphrase Roger Sheringham—albeit out of context), he demonstrated eloquently the immense entertainment value to be derived from murder "judiciously applied."[14] It is to be hoped that appreciation and enjoyment of this gifted and unjustly overlooked writer will become more widespread in years to come.

Appendix

Annotated Checklist of ABC's Books

Brenda Entertains by A.B. Cox. Herbert Jenkins, 1925
>A collection of 27 humorous stories about a garrulous and rather formidable little girl. Most of the stories were revised and reprinted from *Punch* and *The Humorist*.

The Layton Court Mystery by ? Reprinted as "by Anthony Berkeley." Herbert Jenkins, 1925.
>The first Roger Sheringham case. Sheringham and his sidekick, Alec Grierson, investigate the "locked room" death of their host at a country house-party.

Jugged Journalism by A.B. Cox. Herbert Jenkins, 1925.
>A series of 20 comic "lessons" on the art of short-story writing. The sketches are revised and reprinted from *Punch, The Humorist,* and *Passing Show.* The best of the A.B. Cox titles.

The Family Witch: An Essay in Absurdity by A.B. Cox. Herbert Jenkins, 1926.
>Comic fantasy. A young English lord accidentally conjures up a romantically inclined witch—with disconcerting consequences. The book was a reworking of ABC's comic opera of the same title.

The Wintringham Mystery by A.B. Cox. (Newspaper serial) 1926.
>A burlesque of the clichéd country-house mystery, written as a serial for the *Daily Mirror* (1 March–6 April 1926). A young woman disappears during a seance in a rural stately home. ABC revised the novel and republished it, under the pseudonym A. Monmouth Platts, as *Cicely Disappears.*

The Professor on Paws by A.B. Cox. Collins, 1926.
> Comic fantasy. A brilliant scientist's belief in the possibility of biological grafting is vindicated when, following his death, his brain is grafted on to the body of a kitten.

The Wychford Poisoning Case by "the author of *The Layton Court Mystery*" [Anthony Berkeley]. Collins, 1926.
> The second Sheringham case. Roger and Alec Grierson investigate the arsenic poisoning of a provincial businessman. The novel is based on the real-life Maybrick case and ABC's solution endorses one theory of what caused James Maybrick's death.

The Vane Mystery (a.k.a. *Roger Sheringham and the Vane Mystery*) by Anthony Berkeley. Collins, 1927.
> Roger Sheringham matches wits for the first time with Chief Inspector Moresby of Scotland Yard, as both seek to find out who pushed Mrs Vane off a clifftop at Ludmouth. Issued in the United States by Simon and Schuster as *The Mystery of Lover's Cave* (1927).

Mr Priestley's Problem: An Extravaganza in Crime by A.B. Cox. Collins, 1927.
> A burlesque of the thriller genre in which a retiring middle-aged man finds himself the victim of an elaborate murder hoax—and discovers romance in the process. The novel was published by Doubleday in the United States as *The Amateur Crime* (1928). Later reprints bore the Anthony Berkeley byline.

Cicely Disappears by A. Monmouth Platts. John Long, 1927.
> Revised version of *The Wintringham Mystery* (see above).

The Silk Stocking Murders by Anthony Berkeley. Collins, 1928.
> Roger Sheringham investigates the activities of a ruthless serial killer who strangles his victims with their own stockings. Roger has the satisfaction of beating Moresby to the solution.

The Poisoned Chocolates Case by Anthony Berkeley. Collins, 1929.
 Generally regarded as the Berkeley masterpiece, the novel is
 an expansion of the classic short story "The Avenging
 Chance." It finds Roger Sheringham and fellow members of
 the prestigious Crime Circle competing to discover who poisoned the chocolates that killed Joan Bendix. The book marks
 the first appearance of the unlikely looking sleuth, Mr Chitterwick.

The Piccadilly Murder by Anthony Berkeley. Collins, 1929.
 Another outstanding Berkeley mystery (without Sheringham
 this time). Mr Chitterwick witnesses the fatal poisoning of an
 elderly lady in the lounge of a London hotel, and ultimately
 solves the crime.

The Second Shot by Anthony Berkeley. Hodder & Stoughton, 1930.
 Sheringham is called in by an old school-fellow to investigate
 the shooting of an unprincipled rake at a country house-
 party. An expanded version of the short story "Perfect
 Alibi,"*The Second Shot* foreshadowed the author's increasing
 focus on character in the crime novel.

Malice Aforethought: The Story of a Commonplace Crime by Francis
Iles. Mundanus (Gollancz), 1931.
 A dazzling study of the mind of a murderer, based on the
 true-life Armstrong case. A seemingly ineffectual little country doctor eliminates his shrewish wife so he can win the
 hand of an attractive young heiress. His homicidal success
 goes to his head and he plans further revenge killings.

Top Storey Murder by Anthony Berkeley. Hodder & Stoughton,
1931.
 Published by Doubleday in the United States as *Top Story
 Murder*. Sheringham and Moresby team up to investigate the
 strangling of an elderly woman in a shabby block of London
 flats. Moresby sets his sights on the criminal underworld;
 Sheringham prefers to believe the culprit might be found
 within the victim's immediate circle.

Murder in the Basement by Anthony Berkeley. Hodder & Stoughton, 1932.

Moresby investigates the discovery of a pregnant woman's body in the cellar of a suburban London house. Sheringham is able to provide insights into the victim thanks to a short period he has spent as a fill-in schoolmaster at a Surrey prep school. An effective traditional puzzle-story which focuses more than usual on police procedure.

Before the Fact by Francis Iles. Gollancz, 1932.

Another skilled character study which was first published as a serial, *Married to a Murderer*, in the *Daily Express*. This time, the mind of the victim is under the microscope. Lina Aysgarth gradually becomes aware that her easy-going husband is actually an unscrupulous ne'er-do-well whose activities encompass embezzlement, theft and murder. By the end of the book, Lina has realized that she is doomed to be his next victim. *Before the Fact* was filmed (with a modified ending) by Alfred Hitchcock as *Suspicion* (1941), and a revised edition of the book was published by Pan in 1958. The character of Johnnie Aysgarth was inspired by the mass-poisoner William Palmer.

Jumping Jenny by Anthony Berkeley. Hodder & Stoughton, 1933.

Roger Sheringham attends a "Murder" party staged by a popular crime writer and finds himself called on to investigate the hanging of a particularly disagreeable woman guest. *Jumping Jenny* is the prime example of a Berkeley speciality: the "justifiable" murder of a worthless victim by a sympathetic and likeable culprit. One of the best of the Berkeley novels, it was published by Doubleday in the United States as *Dead Mrs Stratton*. (The American edition includes a short biographical study of Sheringham).

Panic Party by Anthony Berkeley. Hodder & Stoughton, 1934.

An underrated Berkeley novel of great interest as a study of a group of people under stress. Roger Sheringham is invited by a former Oxford don to join a mystery cruise, and finds himself and his fellow guests stranded on an uncharted island.

One of the group proves to be a murderer. The last Sheringham novel, *Panic Party* was published by Doubleday in the
United States as *Mr Pidgeon's Island.*

O England! by A.B. Cox. Hamish Hamilton, 1934.
A highly personal analysis of British society, laws and politics, which is now of greatest interest for what it tells us about
its author. The book contains a somewhat idiosyncratic prescription for curing the country's ills.

Trial and Error by Anthony Berkeley. Hodder & Stoughton, 1937.
A shining example of the author's skill in complex characterization and the multiple solution. The terminally ill Mr Todhunter plans and executes a murder (for the good of humanity). He finds himself compelled to prove his guilt when an
innocent man is tried for the crime. Based on the Pelizzioni
case, *Trial and Error* is in many ways more an Iles than a
Berkeley novel, but it features Inspector Moresby and Mr
Chitterwick. It was filmed in 1941 as *Flight from Destiny.*

Not to Be Taken by Anthony Berkeley. Hodder & Stoughton, 1938.
A "cosy" village poisoning tale (rather in the Agatha Christie
mold), and without either Sheringham or Chitterwick, this
novel was written for serialization in *John O'London's Weekly.*
Like *The Wychford Poisoning Case*, it duplicates many aspects
of the Maybrick case. It was published in the United States as
A Puzzle in Poison.

Death in the House by Anthony Berkeley. Hodder & Stoughton,
1939.
The last Berkeley book. Attempts by the British Government
to introduce its highly controversial Indian bill result in the
death of three MPs in the House of Commons itself. With Parliament and the country in an uproar, Under-secretary of
State for India Sir Arthur Linton sets out to solve the mystery.

As for the Woman by Francis Iles. Jarrolds, 1939.
ABC's final published novel, originally planned as the first
part of a trilogy. A naive young man finds himself captivated

by a neurotic married woman; their affair recalls the Thompson-Bywaters and Rattenbury-Stoner murder cases. The novel is an admirable character study, but is much less successful overall than either of its (Iles) predecessors.

A Pocketbook of 100 New Limericks by A.B.C. A.B. Cox Ltd., 1959.
A privately printed 24-page collection of distinctly unremarkable poetic efforts by the author. One limerick is dedicated to Francis Iles.

A Pocketbook of 100 More Limericks by A.B.C. A.B. Cox Ltd., 1960.
More of the same.

The Roger Sheringham Stories by Anthony Berkeley. Edited by Ayresome Johns. Thomas Carnacki, 1994.
A limited edition collection, prepared by George Locke of Ferret Fantasy, which collates all previously published Sheringham short stories together with the Sheringham apocrypha contained in the ABC Archive auctioned in London in 1992. Contains "The Avenging Chance" (a longer-than-usual reprint of the story, taken from ABC's typescript), "White Butterfly," "Perfect Alibi," "The Wrong Jar," "Mr Bearstowe Says" (along with an earlier variant "Razor-Edge" and the radio play "Red Anemones"), the stage play "Temporary Insanity" (based on *The Layton Court Mystery*), the sketch "The Body's Upstairs," miscellaneous contemporary reviews of the early novels, and the short story "Double Bluff" (together with its variant form "Direct Evidence").

Notes

1. Introduction

1. At the time of writing, several of the Berkeley titles have been reprinted by the Black Dagger Press in England. Titles released to date are *The Poisoned Chocolates Case, Top Storey Murder* and *Not to Be Taken*. In 1994, also, a limited edition of a new compendium *The Roger Sheringham Stories* was published (for subscribers) by George Locke of Ferret Fantasy in London.

2. LeRoy Lad Panek, *Watteau's Shepherds: The Detective Novel in Britain, 1914–1940*. Bowling Green, Ohio, 1979, p.111-125; William Bradley Strickland, "Anthony Berkeley Cox," in *Twelve Englishmen of Mystery*, ed. Earl F. Bargainnier. Bowling Green, Ohio, 1984, p.121-141; Charles Shibuk, "Anthony Berkeley," *Dictionary of Literary Biography 77*. Detroit, Michigan, 1987, p. 36-43; Melvyn Barnes, "Anthony Berkeley," in *Twentieth Century Crime and Mystery Writers*, ed. John Reilly. 2nd edition. New York, 1985, p. 68-70.

See also: Howard Haycraft, "Anthony Berkeley Cox." *Wilson Library Bulletin* 14 Dec. 1939, p. 268; Chris Steinbrenner and Otto Penzler, *Encyclopaedia of Mystery and Detection*. New York, 1976, p. 25-27.

3. Nancy Blue Wynne, *An Agatha Christie Chronology*. New York, 1976; Robert Barnard, *A Talent to Deceive: An Appreciation of Agatha Christie*. London, 1980.

4. Julian Symons, *Bloody Murder: From the Detective Story to the Crime Novel. A History*. Harmondsworth, Middlesex, 1974, p. 112.

5. M.J. Turnbull, "The Wonderfully Fallible Roger Sheringham," *Clues: A Journal of Detection* 17 (2), 1996, p. 59-85.

6. Paul R. Moy, "A Bibliography of the Works of Anthony Berkeley Cox (Francis Iles)," *Armchair Detective* 14 (3), 1981, p. 236-238; Ayresome Johns, *The Anthony Berkeley Cox Files: Notes towards a Bibliography*. London, 1993. See also Barnes, p. 68-69; John Cooper and B.A. Pike, *Detective Fiction: The Collector's Guide*. Taunton, 1988, p. 24-27.

7. As an added bonus to the collector, each copy of Johns's remarkable bibliography boasts a short, original typescript from the ABC archive.

8. Anthony Berkeley Cox, *The Roger Sheringham Stories*, ed. Ayresome Johns. London, 1994.

2. Anthony Berkeley Cox (1893–1971)

1. Johns, p. 30-32.

2. As Ayresome Johns (p. 3) has pointed out, ABC is "an author about whom there seem to be more mysteries than in the books he created." What biographical and genealogical detail I have managed to unearth has been collated from a number of sources, including his birth, death and marriage certificates; his will (dated 25 Aug. 1969); an obituary in the *Times* (11 March 1971); the St Catherine's House Indexes; Johns, *passim*; Barnes, p. 68; and (in particular) the record of an interview with Celia and Norman Down (6 July 1995).

3. *Victoria History of the Counties of England: Hertfordshire*, Vol 2. London, 1923, p. 447-448.

4. The Family Tree is now in the possession of ABC's niece, Celia Down. Ehret was born at Heidelberg, Germany, in 1708, and settled in England in 1736. Befriended by the Duchess of Portland and Sir Hans Sloane (among others), he won fame as a draughtsman, teacher and collector of plant specimens, published a standard work on the subject, and founded the 'Chelsea Physick Gardens' in London. He died at Chelsea in 1770. Ehret's son George died at Watford in 1786.

Ray Desmond, *Dictionary of British and Irish Botanists and Horticulturalists, including Plant Collectors, Flower Painters and Garden Designers*. Revised edition. London, 1994; Celia Down, letter to the author, 31 July 1995.

5. It is tempting to speculate on the extent to which ABC's analysis of the tensions between the plebeian doctor and his aristocratic wife in *Malice Aforethought* may have drawn on memories of his parents' relationship. The class divisions between the Crewstantons ("one of the most important families in North Devonshire") and the socially "inferior" Bickleighs clearly had a parallel in the Iles-Cox alliance. In fairness, of course, Alfred Cox was no Dr Bickleigh, as his inventive flair indicates.

See Francis Iles, *Malice Aforethought: The Story of a Commonplace Crime*. London, 1931, p. 6-8, 29-30, 33-34.

6. Sybil M. Iles, *The School of Life: A Study in the Discipline of Circumstance*. London, 1905; interview with Celia and Norman Down.

7. Interview with Celia and Norman Down; *The Sherborne Register* 1550-1950. 4th ed., n.d., p. 255.

8. Interview with Celia and Norman Down.

9. Francis Iles, *As for the Woman*. New York, 1939, p. 24-25.

10. *As for the Woman*, p. 31.

11. Johns, p. 22; *Grand Magazine* Sept. 1913, p. 490.

12. In the 1930s, Howard Haycraft speculated (incorrectly) that ABC may have trained as a lawyer, on the strength of the detailed knowledge of courtroom procedure evident in *Trial and Error* and *Malice Aforethought*.

Haycraft 1939, p. 268; details from dust jacket of A.B. Cox, *O England*. London, 1934.

13. Johns, p. 22; *O England*, p. 7-10; Haycraft 1939, p. 268; interview with Celia and Norman Down.

14. Details from British Civil Records, ABC's will and divorce decree (dated 16 November 1931); *O England*, p. 17; Johns, p. 28.

In the Berkeley novel *Jumping Jenny*, Roger Sheringham seems to be speaking for his creator when he fervently concurs that "our marriage-laws are all on the wrong lines. Marriage oughtn't to be easy and divorce difficult; it ought to be just the other way about." Anthony Berkeley, *Jumping Jenny*. Harmondsworth, Middlesex, 1941 [1933], p. 13.

15. Interview with Celia and Norman Down.

16. *O England*, p. 144-145.

17. *Jumping Jenny*, p. 35.

18. [Anthony Berkeley], *The Wychford Poisoning Case*. London, 1926, p. 124-127. ABC's sardonic attitude to women persisted throughout his life. Years later, he observed caustically: "really nice girls do not go to bed with strange men on a couple of hours' acquaintance (I have this on impeccable female authority); they wait at least a week." *Manchester Guardian*, 17 July 1969.

19. Johns, p. 17.

20. Johns, p. 26-27.

21. Cynthia Cox was also a member of the Gnats and played the female lead in "The Family Witch." ABC's handwritten score and libretto is in the possession of his niece.

22. Johns, p. 28-29; *Times*, 31 May 1928.

23. *Punch*, 28 March 1923.

24. Robert Graves and Alan Hodge, *The Long Weekend: A Social History of Great Britain, 1918–1939*. London, 1985 [1940.], p. 300; LeRoy Lad

Panek, *An Introduction to the Detective Story*, Bowling Green, Ohio, 1987, p. 120.

25. Robert Barnard, "The English Detective Story," in *Whodunit? A Guide to Crime, Suspense and Spy Fiction*, ed. H.R.F. Keating. New York, 1982, p. 30.

26. Panek 1987, p. 120-122.

27. See Sayers's introductions to *Great Stories of Detection, Mystery and Horror*. First, second and third series. London, 1928, 1931 and 1934; and her introduction to the Everyman's Library compilation, *Tales of Detection*. London, 1936. ABC and Sayers were keen readers of each other's books. A presentation copy of *The Second Shot* from Sayers's own library bears the Berkeley inscription "Take ye in one another's washing." (The item in question was advertised by the Ulysses Bookshop, London, in 1994.)

28. *Sunday Times*, 18 April 1954; 24 April 1955; *Manchester Guardian* 6 Dec. 1957.

29. Julian Symons, *Bloody Murder: From the Detective Story to the Crime Novel*. Harmondsworth, Middlesex, 1974, p. 110.

30. Interview with Celia and Norman Down.

31. Details from ABC's will; interview with Celia and Norman Down.

32. *Times Literary Supplement*, 10 March 1978; *Times*, 11 March 1971; Johns, p. 28; Haycraft 1939, p. 268.

33. *Times* 11 March and 12 Oct. 1971.

34. Interview with Celia and Norman Down.

35. John Dickson Carr, "The Jury Box," *Ellery Queen's Mystery Magazine* July 1972, p. 87-88.

36. Moy, p. 236. Ayresome Johns, in his introduction to *The Roger Sheringham Stories* (p. xv), cites a tantalizing rumor. During or shortly after World War II, ABC attempted to repeat his Francis Iles coup and published a new novel under yet another pseudonym. To date, no one has been able to verify whether such a work ever existed. If it did, the "mystery book" is not among the writer's own collection of his publications now held by his relatives.

37. ABC's many grievances included what he believed to be the exorbitant conveyancing costs he incurred in his property acquisitions. As a new farm-owner (Linton Hills), he bombarded *The Spectator* on one occasion, claiming that a 10-pound solicitor's bill for a simple transaction represented "yet another" instance of the "discouragement" being

offered agriculture in England: "If I am compelled eventually to pay this rapacious charge, it will mean that, reckoning a normal rate of interest, this land will have to be worked for about eighteen months just to pay the costs of acquiring it, before I can get a penny out of it myself. What inducement is this to farm?" (*The Spectator* 29 Aug. 1931).

38. *Times* 14 Oct. 1937.

39. Johns, p. 23.

40. Philip Ziegler, *King Edward VIII: The Official Biography*. London, 1990, p. 319, 344-345; Johns, Addendum.

41. Shibuk, p. 43; Haycraft 1939, p. 268; *Sunday Times*, 14 March 1971.

42. Interview with Celia and Norman Down.

43. Doug Greene, "Yet Another Note on the Least-known Member of the Detection Club (and Some Others)," *Crime and Detective Stories* 12 Nov. 1989, p. 42.

44. Greene, p. 42; *Sunday Times* 14 March 1971; Gwen Robyns, *The Mystery of Agatha Christie*. New York, 1978, p. 107; interview with Celia and Norman Down.

45. *Times Literary Supplement* 10 March 1978.

46. Details from ABC's will.

47. *Times Literary Supplement* 10 March 1978.

48. *Sunday Times* 14 March 1971.

49. According to Christianna Brand, quoted by Shibuk, p. 42-43; interview with Celia and Norman Down.

50. Interview with Celia and Norman Down.

51. Interview with Celia and Norman Down; details from ABC's death certificate.

52. *Manchester Guardian* 11 March 1971; *Daily Telegraph* 10 March 1971; *Times* 11 March 1971; *Sunday Times* 14 March 1971; *Ellery Queen's Mystery Magazine* July 1972, p. 87-88.

53. Shibuk, p. 43; ABC's will.

3. A.B. Cox, Humorist

1. Haycraft 1939, p. 268.

2. Moy, p. 236-237.

3. *Punch* 30 July, 1924. Revised and reprinted in A.B. Cox, *Jugged Journalism*. London, 1925, p. 13.

4. Johns, p. 17.

5. *Punch* 1 Nov. 1922; 28 Feb. 1923; 11 April 1923.

6. According to Celia Down, the Brenda characters had real-life counterparts. Mr. Smith was the author's brother, Stephen, and Brenda was his young sister-in-law. Interview with Celia and Norman Down.

7. See Johns, p. 18, for detail.

8. *Jugged Journalism*, p. 16-19.

9. Johns, p. 18, 20, 26, 27.

10. For a listing of the *Down Our Road* sketches, see Johns, p. 18, 26, 27.

11. Johns, p. 28.

12. ABC based the exuberant Lady Angela on his sister, Cynthia, who played the role in the stage production of *The Family Witch*. Interview with Celia and Norman Down.

13. *Times Literary Supplement* 11 Feb. 1926.

14. *New York Times* 12 June 1927; *Times Literary Supplement* 12 Aug. 1926.

15. Johns, p. 17-18.

16. Johns, p. 24.

17. Panek 1979, p. 114.

18. Anthony Berkeley [A.B. Cox], *Mr. Priestley's Problem: An Extravaganza in Crime*. Harmondsworth, Middlesex, 1948 [1927], p. 70.

19. Shibuk, p. 38-29.

20. *Times* 28 March 1928.

21. *Sunday Times* 14 March 1971; interview with Celia and Norman Down. ABC bequeathed all his musical copyrights and royalties to Norman Down, who cites the gesture as a typically "Coxian" joke. ABC also took credit for the incidental music used in a broadcast of *Trial and Error* (by the BBC in 1957), and claimed that some of it was reused on Alfred Hitchcock's TV series.

22. *Times* 31 May 1928; Johns, p. 29.

23. Johns, p. 12; *Times Literary Supplement* 10 March 1978.

24. "I know a man who does not like the work of Mr. P.G. Wodehouse," ABC once wrote. "You disbelieve me? I swear it is true. I spend my days wondering what can be done about him. It would be more instructive, I think, to write an essay on him than on the art of Mr. P.G. Wodehouse. . . ." He affectionately parodied the comic master in a number of sketches (including the sprightly "Revolution from Inside," *Passing Show* 29 Sept. 1923) and clearly strove (with only qualified success) to emulate Wodehouse's "glorious gift of invariably fitting the

impossibly right word into the hilariously right place" in his own writing. The two writers were well acquainted and shared a strong enthusiasm for the detective story. A letter exists from Wodehouse to ABC, in which the former gratefully acknowledges receipt of a copy of *Trial and Error*, and then goes on to recommend the work of Georgette Heyer, Q. Patrick and E.R. Punshon. Wodehouse expresses relief that S.S. Van Dine seems to have stopped writing and confides that, fond though he is of Dorothy L. Sayers's books, he has found *Busman's Honeymoon* hard to take. ("I shuddered every time a rustic came on the scene.")

Daily Telegraph 26 April and 18 Oct. 1935; letter from P.G. Wodehouse to ABC, 16 Oct. 1937 (made available by Celia Down).

25. Johns, p. 18.

4. Anthony Berkeley (I): Roger Sheringham

1. *Punch* 28 March 1923.

2. *Jugged Journalism*, p. 34.

3. Strickland, p. 123.

4. Johns, p. 19. Johns also notes that the ABC archive contains an unpublished seven-page romantic dialogue, "Man Proposes," signed "Anthony Berkeley," and possibly written as early as 1920.

5. Haycraft 1939, p. 268.

6. [Anthony Berkeley], *The Layton Court Mystery*. London, 1925, p. v.

7. Quoted in Haycraft 1939, p. 268.

8. Panek 1979, p. 112.

9. Strickland, p. 124.

10. Panek 1979, p. 113.

11. Anthony Berkeley, "Concerning Roger Sheringham," in *Dead Mrs Stratton*. New York, 1933, p. viii.

12. ABC's first two detective novels, *The Layton Court Mystery* and *The Wychford Poisoning Case*, were originally published anonymously. They were reprinted as "by Anthony Berkeley."

13. *Sunday Times* 22 Aug. 1954.

14. Quoted in Haycraft 1939, p. 268.

15. J.S. Fletcher, "The Maybrick Trial," in *Great Unsolved Crimes*. London, 1938, p. 95.

16. *The Wychford Poisoning Case*, p. v, 144.

17. Shibuk, p. 38.

18. *New York Evening Post* 26 April 1930. "There ought to be a new set of sumptuary laws passed and a public spanker appointed in every town," argues Sheringham. He proposes rationing the "modern girl" to one lipstick a month, 20 cigarettes per week, and 4 damns a day. He does not interfere when Alec spanks Sheila (Alec believes she "deserves a whack"), and he chastises her himself with a rolled-up magazine.

19. Panek 1979, p. 117-118.

20. Jacques Barzun and Wendell Hertig Taylor, *A Catalogue of Crime.* New York, 1971, p. 57.

21. Alec Grierson disappears after the Wychford investigation, and reappears only in the recently published short story "Double Bluff"/ "Direct Evidence." A fragment of an unpublished (presumably uncompleted) novel exists in which Alec and Roger again discuss a case over breakfast. (See Johns, p. 25.) In *The Silk Stocking Murders*, we learn that Alec has gone out to Brazil.

22. Anthony Berkeley, *The Vane Mystery.* London, 1927, p. 285.

23. Shibuk, p. 39; Strickland, p. 126.

24. *Boston Transcript* 6 Oct. 1928. *The Times Literary Supplement* 7 June 1928 criticized ABC/Berkeley for laying on the horrors "with a trowel."

25. Anthony Berkeley, *The Silk Stocking Murders.* New York, 1928, p. 17, 22.

Pejorative remarks about Jews abound in Golden Age detective fiction, and the ABC books are no exception. There are fewer anti-Semitic remarks in the Sheringham cases than in the Wimsey or Hercule Poirot stories, but ABC still feels compelled to rank Jews with prunes and tapioca as the things Sheringham detests most in the world (in *The Layton Court Mystery*, p. 264). Elsewhere, an intensely disagreeable newspaper tycoon is described as "a nasty piece of work . . . American German Jew, with a dash of anything else unpleasant thrown in" (*Trial and Error*, p. 66), and an unattractive financier is obviously means to be Jewish (in *The Wintringham Mystery/Cicely Disappears*). ABC does compensate a little in *Not to Be Taken*, where he ridicules a fanatically anti-Semitic Nazi cook, but his last published story, "It Takes Two to Make a Hero" (by Francis Iles), includes an unnecessary reference to an ugly old Jewish shopkeeper.

26. Agatha Christie mildly parodies *The Silk Stocking Murders* in *Partners in Crime* (1920). "I wish we could befriend a clergyman's daugh-

ter," declares Tuppence Beresford of "Blunt's Brilliant Detectives." "You are getting ready to be Roger Sheringham, I see," responds her husband, Tommy, moments before a "clergyman's daughter" arrives to enlist the couple's aid. Agatha Christie, *Partners in Crime*. London, 1958 [1929], p. 147.

27. Ellery Queen, *In the Queen's Parlour and Other Leaves from the Editor's Notebook*. London, 1957, p. 89; *101 Years' Entertainment: The Great Detective Stories, 1841-1941*, ed. Ellery Queen. Boston, 1943, p. 436.

28. Symons, p. 112.

29. Anthony Berkeley, *The Poisoned Chocolates Case and The Avenging Chance*, with a new denouement by Christianna Brand. San Francisco, 1979. For contemporary reviews of the novel, see the introduction to *The Roger Sheringham Stories*, p. xii-xiv.

30. "Perfect Alibi" was first published by the *Radio Times*, 1 Aug. 1930. It was reprinted in condensed form, and with the victim's name changed to Eric Southwood, in the *Evening Standard* 11 March 1953.

31. Panek 1979, p. 119.

32. *Times Literary Supplement* 25 Dec. 1930.

A more recent "retrospective" review of *The Second Shot* is more enthusiastic. "What 'Berkeley' worked out was a way to put the Pirandello atmosphere of the purist mystery to work in his plot," writes J.M. Purcell, noting that the author "puts the traditional unbelievabilities of the form to use as part of the actual murder scheme." By providing a Watsonian narrator "who reports data" without properly interpreting it for the reader, ABC/Berkeley cleverly "breaks the Jamesian rule about an adequately perceptive narrator for serious fiction." "Retrospective Reviews," *Armchair Detective* 9(3), 1976.

33. Shibuk, p. 40.

34. Shibuk, p. 40.

35. Barzun and Taylor, p. 55.

36. *Times Literary Supplement* 31 Aug. 1933.

37. One critic has applauded ABC/Berkeley's employment of "one of the most effective colons in literature" in the cunning scene in which we are supposedly shown the murder being committed. R. Philmore, "Inquest on Detective Stories," Part 2, *Discovery* Sept. 1938.

38. The story was a contribution to Dorothy L. Sayers's "Detective Cavalcade" series. *Evening Standard* 28 Aug. 1936.

39. Johns judges "The Wrong Jar" an excellent story, arguably even better than "The Avenging Chance." Johns p. 25.

40. The ABC archive contains notes and a synopsis for a projected novel (a "seaside story") along the lines of "Red Anemones" and "Mr Bearstowe Says." Johns, p. 29.

41. *The Roger Sheringham Stories*, p. 70-93; Johns, p. 21-22.

42. *The Roger Sheringham Stories*, p. vi-viii, 1-53; Johns, p. 21, 29.

43. Johns, p. 25-26.

44. Johns, p. 25.

45. In *Ask a Policeman*, the Home Secretary insists that Roger's background gives him an advantage over the police in interviewing and probing among bishops and the landed gentry. (Sayers notes that Moresby is decidedly skeptical of this.)

46. *The Layton Court Mystery*, p. 11, 12.

47. *Murder in the Basement*, p. 65.

48. Strickland, p. 125.

49. Strickland, p. 125-126.

50. Dorothy L. Sayers, *Have His Carcase*. London, 1932, p. 431.

51. Shibuk, p. 38.

5. Anthony Berkeley (II): Moresby, Chitterwick and Others

1. Alec seems to be following the example of another "Watson," Captain Hastings (Hercule Poirot's compatriot), who went out to Argentina after finding true love in Agatha Christie's *Murder on the Links* (1923).

2. *The Vane Mystery*, p. 26-27.

3. Panek 1979, p. 114.

4. Shibuk, p. 39.

5. *The Poisoned Chocolates Case*, p. 12.

6. Alzina Stone Dale and Barbara Sloan Hendershott, *Mystery Reader's Walking Guide to London*. London, 1987, p. 101.

7. Anthony Berkeley, *The Piccadilly Murder*. New York, 1930 [1929], p. 1.

8. Strickland, p. 136.

9. Shibuk, p. 42; Strickland, p. 136-137. When ABC died, the *Manchester Guardian* (11 March 1971) singled out *Trial and Error* for praise as ". . . a classic, its plot a masterpiece of symmetry and comic irony."

10. Anthony Berkeley, introduction to Penguin edition of *Trial and Error*. Harmondsworth, Middlesex, 1947 [1937], p. vii-ix.

11. Johns, p. 28.

12. Panek 1979, p. 114-116.

13. Anthony Berkeley, *Trial and Error*. London, 1937, p. 526-527.

14. *The Poisoned Chocolates Case*, p. 6; *The Piccadilly Murder*, p. 7; *Trial and Error*, p. 267.

15. Panek 1979, p. 115.

16. Anthony Berkeley, *Not to Be Taken*. Harmondsworth, Middlesex, 1946 [1938], p. 220-222.

17. *Not to Be Taken*, p. 10.

18. See *New Statesman and Nation* 6 Aug. 1938; *Books* 11 Sept. 1938; *Spectator* 19 Aug. 1938; *Manchester Guardian* 2 Aug. 1938.

19. *Spectator* 23 June, 1939; Barzun and Taylor, p. 55.

20. Anthony Berkeley, *Death in the House*. New York, 1939, p. 22.

21. *Death in the House*, p. 99-100.

A third serial was planned for *John O'London's Weekly*, called "Poison Pipe," but it never materialized.

22. The writer attempted to dramatize "Publicity Heroine" in the late 1930s. The ABC Archive contains a 60-page fragment which includes the completed Act I, a few pages of Act II, and numerous notes and drafts which suggest that ABC may have also contemplated expanding the story into a novel. Johns, p. 28.

23. Anthony Berkeley, "The Policeman Only Taps Once," in Detection Club, *Six Against the Yard*. New York, 1989 [1936], p. 76.

24. Johns, p. 28-29.

25. Johns, p. 21.

26. Johns, p. 28; Janet Morgan, *Agatha Christie: A Biography*. London, 1984, p. 195.

Behind the Screen was translated into French, and appeared in *L'Humoristique* , as "Derriere Le Paravent," in February-March 1931.

27. Morgan, p. 195-196.

Johns notes that a small archive of material to do with the project sold at Sothebys for 7,500 pounds in December 1992. The material included letters by Christie, Sayers and Ronald Knox, and carbon typescripts and synopses by Sayers, E.C. Bentley and ABC. Johns, p. 28.

28. Morgan, p. 195; Johns, p. 29

29. Morgan, p. 195-197.

30. Johns, p. 29.

31. Detection Club, *The Floating Admiral*. London, 1981 [1931], p. 5; *Times Literary Supplement* 10 Dec. 1931.

32. Detection Club, *Ask a Policeman*. New York, 1983 [1933], p. 174.

33. *New York Evening Post* 24 June 1933; *Books* 18 June 1933; *New York Times* 18 June 1933; *Times Literary Supplement* 27 April 1933.

34. *Manchester Guardian* 5 July 1957; 4 Oct. 1957.

35. Panek 1979, p. 125.

36. *Sunday Times* 24 April 1955.

37. Symons, p. 112.

38. Barnes, p. 70.

39. Johns, p. 30.

40. Anthony Berkeley, *The Second Shot*. New York, 1930, p. 5-6.

41. Barzun and Taylor, p. 55.

6. Francis Iles

1. *Sunday Times* 24 April 1955.

2. *The Second Shot*, p. 5.

3. *Sunday Times* 14 March 1971.

4. Barnes, p. 70.

5. *Sunday Times* 14 March 1971; Symons, p. 138.

6. Howard Haycraft, *Murder for Pleasure: The Life and Times of the Detective Story*. New York, 1941, p. 148.

7. Haycraft 1941, p. 148.

8. Johns, p. 30.

9. For a rundown of the "Who Is Francis Iles?" debate, see Johns, p. 30-31; see also Jon L. Breen, *What About Murder? (1981–1991): A Guide to Books about Mystery and Detective Fiction*. Metuchen, 1993, p. 2.

10. Francis Iles, foreword to *As for the Woman*. New York, 1939.

11. Haycraft 1939, p. 268; Johns, p. 30-31.

12. Quoted in Shibuk, p. 42.

13. Haycraft 1941, p. 147.

14. *Punch* 28 March 1923.

15. Francis Iles, *Malice Aforethought: The Story of a Commonplace Crime*. London, 1931, p. 1.

16. Panek, 1979, p. 120.

17. *Malice Aforethought*, p. 26.

18. *Times Literary Supplement* 10 March 1978.

19. *Times Literary Supplement* 19 March 1931; *New York Times* 7 June, 1931; *Saturday Review* 28 Feb. 1931; *English Review* Oct. 1931.

20. Shibuk, p. 40; Strickland, p. 132.

21. Quoted in Shibuk, p. 40; Symons, p. 138.

22. Art Bourgeau, *The Mystery Lover's Companion*. New York, 1986, p. 160.

23. Strickland, p. 131.

24. *Times Literary Supplement* 10 March 1978.

25. *Malice Aforethought*, p. 84-85.

26. Strickland, p. 132-133.

27. H.R.F. Keating, *Crime and Mystery: The 100 Best Books*. London, 1987, p. 45.

28. Francis Iles, *Before the Fact*. London, 1932, p. 1.

29. *Bookman*, Jan. 1933; *New Statesman & Nation* 25 June 1932; *Saturday Review* 10 Dec. 1932; *Times Literary Supplement* 7 July 1932.

30. Haycraft 1941, p. 145; Keating, p. 46; Shibuk, p. 40.

31. Panek, 1979, p. 121; Strickland, p. 135-136.

32. *Times Literary Supplement* 10 March 1978.

33. Shibuk, p. 42.

34. Keating, p. 45-46.

35. *Suspicion* was refilmed for television in the 1980s, with Anthony Andrews as Johnnie Aysgarth. The telemovie stuck closely to the Hitchcock screenplay rather than to the Iles original.

36. Francis Iles, *Before the Fact*, rev. ed. London, 1958, p. 41, 71, 101, 154.

37. *Times Literary Supplement* 10 March 1978.

38. Keating, p. 46.

39. *Times Literary Supplement* 10 March 1978.

40. *Times Literary Supplement* 7 April 1978.

41. *Manchester Guardian* 4 Aug. 1939.

42. Moy, p. 236.

43. As noted earlier, ABC provided readers with a partial self-portrait and evocations of his mother, brother Stephen and sister Cynthia in the opening chapters of *As for the Woman*.

44. Francis Iles, *As for the Woman*, New York, 1939, p. 166.

45. *As for the Woman*, p. 221.

46. *New York Times* 29 Oct. 1939; *Saturday Review* 28 Oct. 1939; *Spectator* 28 July 1939; *Canadian Forum* Dec. 1939; *John O'London's Weekly* 28 July 1939.

47. Shibuk, p. 42.

48. Moy, p. 236; *Times Literary Supplement* 10 March 1978.

49. Francis Iles, "Dark Journey," in *To the Queen's Taste*, ed. Ellery Queen. New York, 1946 [1934].

50. Francis Iles, "Outside the Law," *Strand* July 1934. "Outside the Law" was reprinted several times, sometimes as an Anthony Berkeley creation (rather incongruously, given the story's unrelieved seriousness).

51. Francis Iles, "It Takes Two to Make a Hero," *Saturday Book 3* 1943.

52. Francis Iles, "Sense of Humour," *Strand* Oct. 1935.

53. Johns, p. 23, 28, 29.

Johns notes that a series of seven murder stories, "written and narrated by Francis Iles," aired on radio in the second half of 1932. Collectively titled "By the Neck," they may have included the radiologues described here.

54. A.B. Cox, "The Right to Kill," *The Democrat* 30 Dec. 1922.

55. Johns, p. 21-23.

56. Francis Iles, "Close Season in Polchester," in *Parody Party*, ed. Leonard Russell. London, 1936; Francis Iles, "Eastern Love Song," in *Press Gang: Crazy World Chronicle*, ed. Leonard Russell. London, 1937. (Other contributors to *Press Gang* included Dilys Powell, Hilaire Belloc, John Betjeman, Ronald Knox and E.M. Delafield.)

57. *Manchester Guardian* 2 Nov. 1956.

58. *Sunday Times* 14 March, 1971.

7. Nonfiction: True Crime, Book Reviews and Politics

1. *The Second Shot*, p. 6.

2. Francis Iles, "The Rattenbury Case," in Detection Club, *The Anatomy of Murder*, London, 1936. Reprinted in *More Anatomy of Murder*, New York, 1990, p. 124.

3. "The Rattenbury Case," p. 126.

4. Panek 1979, p. 114.

5. *The Silk Stocking Murders*, p. 29.

6. *The Wychford Poisoning Case*, p. 30-31, 51.

7. Johns, p. 26.

8. *The Wychford Poisoning Case*, p. 31.

9. Francis Iles, "Was Crippen a Murderer?" in *Great Unsolved Crimes*, London, 1938, p. 15-22; Colin Wilson and Patricia Pitman, *Encyclopaedia of Murder*, New York, 1962, p. 169.

10. Anthony Berkeley, "Who Killed Madame X?" in *Great Unsolved Crimes*, p. 112-118.

11. Francis Iles, "Mrs Rattenbury," *Strand* May 1943, p. 78.

12. Other contributors to *The Anatomy of Murder* were Dorothy L. Sayers ("The Murder of Julia Wallace"), Freeman Wills Crofts (on the Lakey tragedy in New Zealand), John Rhode (on Constance Kent), Helen Simpson ("The Death of Henry Kinder"), Margaret Cole ("The Case of Adelaide Bartlett") and E.R. Punshon (on Landru).

13. ABC/Iles notes: "It is said that this was the first occasion in British criminal history in which two persons, put on trial jointly for the same murder, have not tried to save themselves by putting the blame on the other." "Mrs Rattenbury," p. 79.

14. "The Rattenbury Case," p. 138.

15. "The Rattenbury Case," p. 134.

16. "The Rattenbury Case," p. 60-61, 120.

17. "The Rattenbury Case," p. 150.

18. ABC/Iles succeeded Eric Forbes-Boyd as regular crime reviewer for the *Sunday Times* in 1953. Edgar Wallace's daughter, Pat, took over the role when ABC transferred to the *Guardian*, and Julian Symons inherited the column two years later.

19. *Manchester Guardian* 2 Nov. 1956, 5 July 1957.

Early in his career, ABC confessed (in a sketch titled "Detective Marion," *London Opinion* 25 July 1925): "I think I must be the sort of reader that every writer of detective stories goes down on his knees and prays for . . . Every night I am, I fear, utterly without guile. When there is a simply overwhelming mass of evidence all pointing at one man, I invariably suspect him of having committed the murder in the first chapter. That, I have always thought, is what evidence is for."

20. *Manchester Guardian* 4 Oct. 1957; 20 May 1960.

21. *Time and Tide* 11 Feb. 1933; *Daily Telegraph* 8 Nov. 1935; 3 Jan. 1936; *Sunday Times* 18 April 1954; 31 Oct. 1954; *Manchester Guardian* 7 Dec. 1956; 6 Dec. 1957.

Sayers responded with characteristic wit to ABC/Iles's criticism of her pet sleuth. In a letter to Helen Simpson, she observed:

> Mr Iles
> Should be debagged in the middle
> of St Giles
> For calling Peter Wimsey
> Flimsy.

Dorothy L. Sayers, *The Letters of Dorothy L. Sayers 1899–1936: The Making of a Detective Novelist*. London: Hodder & Stoughton, 1995, p. 360.

22. *Daily Telegraph* 1 Nov. 1935; 6 March, 1936; *Sunday Times* 3 Jan. 1954; 1 May 1955; *Manchester Guardian* 2 Aug. 1957; 14 Nov. 1958.

23. *Manchester Guardian* 1 March, 1957; 4 Oct. 1957; 29 April, 1960; 29 July 1960: 26 May 1967.

24. *Manchester Guardian* 6 Dec. 1957; 2 May 1958.

25. *Daily Telegraph* 3 Jan. 1936; *Sunday Times* 18 April 1954; *Manchester Guardian* 2 Nov. 1956; 4 Jan. 1957; 2 Aug. 1957; 26 Aug. 1960.

26. *Manchester Guardian* 1 Feb. 1957; 5 July 1957; 6 Sept. 1957; 6 Dec. 1957; 9 June 1967.

In ABC's view, Hillary Waugh's *The Young Prey* highlighted the fundamental difference between the British and American approaches to the crime novel: to the British "impersonal cold-blooded proof" is everything, to Americans no case can stand up without a confession. ("It does not occur to anyone to try to prove a case against the guilty man.") *Manchester Guardian* 2 July 1970.

27. *Manchester Guardian* 2 Aug. 1957; 6 Sept. 1957; 4 Oct. 1957; 23 Sept. 1960; 14 April 1967; 26 May 1967; 14 Aug. 1969; 28 May 1970; 24 Sept. 1970; *Daily Telegraph* 11 April 1936.

28. *Manchester Guardian* 4 Jan. 1957; 7 June 1957.

29. *Daily Telegraph* 17 Nov. 1933; 8 Dec. 1933; 29 Dec. 1933; 5 Jan. 1934.

A series of statements on critics' responsibility drew support from an (arguably) unexpected quarter—Kenneth Nielsen, the third party in ABC's divorce action against his first wife. Nielsen described himself as "a grateful member of that public on whose behalf Mr. Iles was apparently ready to sacrifice friendship to duty." Nielsen fervently hoped that Iles would gain many new friends "who find in his provocative outspokenness a relief from the sickly stream of soothing syrup of 'those others.'" *Daily Telegraph* 5 Jan. 1934.

30. Francis Iles, "Rewards and Reviewers," *Time and Tide* 21 March 1936.

31. *As for the Woman*, p. 14, 90.

32. *Before the Fact*, p. 124, 196, 278.

33. *O England*, p. 15.

34. *O England*, p. 22-23.

35. *O England*, p. 144-147.

36. *Times Literary Supplement* 24 Jan. 1935.

37. Johns, Addendum.

38. Ziegler, p. 344-345.

8. Conclusion

1. *Before the Fact*, p. 255.

2. Panek 1979, p. 111, 112, 119-124; Strickland, p. 131, 139, 140.

3. Barnes, p. 70.

4. Panek 1979, p. 122-125; *Jumping Jenny*, p. 134.

5. Panek 1979, p. 122-123.

6. Panek 1979, p. 124-125.

7. Like his sympathetic victims, ABC's totally unsympathetic murderers are few in number—most notable are Johnnie Aysgarth, the professional burglar in *Top Storey Murder*, Major Cresswell in "White Butterfly," the crazed idealist of *Death in the House*, and the deranged perpetrator of *The Silk Stocking Murders*.

8. Isobel goes on to declare (a la Sheringham): "Believe me, *hundreds* of people walking about today have put somebody out of the way in their time. Why, it's as easy as falling into a bog. Just a nudge with the elbow as they're walking along the edge of a cliff . . ." *Before the Fact*, p. 273, 282.

9. Panek 1979, p. 116.

10. Panek 1979, p. 119.

11. Panek 1979, p. 121.

12. Strickland, p. 123-124.

13. Strickland, p. 124.

14. Sheringham expresses himself acutely aware of the "value of nonsense, judiciously applied" in *The Layton Court Mystery*, p. 23.

Select Bibliography

Primary Sources

Editions of ABC's Books, Short Stories, etc. Cited in the Text

This listing does not include the many sketches mentioned in the text (for detail see the Johns bibliography), or ABC's many book reviews in the *Daily Telegraph* (1933–36), *Time and Tide* (1932–33), *John O'London's Weekly* (1938), *Sunday Times* (1953–56) and *Manchester Guardian* (1956–70).

Berkeley, Anthony "The Avenging Chance." In *Tales of Detection*. Ed. Dorothy L. Sayers. London: Dent, 1936.

——. *Dead Mrs Stratton* (U.S. edition of *Jumping Jenny*). New York: Doubleday, 1933.

——. *Death in the House.* New York: Doubleday, 1939.

——. *Jumping Jenny.* Harmondsworth, Middlesex: Penguin, 1941 [1933].

[——.] *The Layton Court Mystery.* London: Herbert Jenkins, 1925.

——. "Mr Bearstowe Says." *Saturday Book 3.* London: Hutchinson, 1943.

——. *Mr Pidgeon's Island* (U.S. edition of *Panic Party*). New York: Doubleday, 1934.

——"Mr Simpson Goes to the Dogs." *Strand* June 1934.

——. *Murder in the Basement.* New York: Doubleday, 1932.

——. *Not to Be Taken.* Harmondsworth, Middlesex: Penguin, 1946 [1938].

——."Perfect Alibi." *Radio Times* 1 Aug. 1930. Revised version *Evening Standard* 11 March 1953.

——. *The Piccadilly Murder.* New York: Doubleday, 1929.

——. *The Poisoned Chocolates Case.* New York: Doubleday, 1929.

——. *The Poisoned Chocolates Case and the Avenging Chance*, with a new denouement by Christianna Brand. San Francisco: University of California, 1979.

——. Publicity Heroine." In *Missing from Their Homes.* London: Hutchinson, 1936.

——. *The Roger Sheringham Stories*. Ed. Ayresome Johns. London: Thomas Carnacki, 1994.

——. *The Second Shot*. New York: Doubleday, 1930.

——. *The Silk Stocking Murders*. New York: Doubleday, 1928.

——. *Top Story Murder* (U.S. edition of *Top Storey Murder*). New York: Grosset & Dunlap, 1931.

——. *Trial and Error*. London: Hodder & Stoughton, 1937; Harmondsworth, Middlesex: Penguin, 1947.

——. *The Vane Mystery*. London: Collins, c. 1930 [1927].

——. White Butterfly." *Ellery Queen's Mystery Magazine* Dec. 1981 [1936].

——. Who Killed Madame X?" In *Great Unsolved Crimes*. London: Hutchinson, 1938.

——. "The Wrong Jar." In *Detective Stories of Today*. Ed. Raymond Postgate. London: Faber, 1940.

[——.] *The Wychford Poisoning Case*. London: Collins, 1926.

Cox, A.B. *Brenda Entertains*. London: Herbert Jenkins, 1925.

——. *The Family Witch: An Essay in Absurdity*. London: Herbert Jenkins, 1926.

——. *Jugged Journalism*. London: Herbert Jenkins, 1925.

——. *Mr Priestley's Problem: An Extravaganza in Crime*. Reprinted as "by Anthony Berkeley." Harmondsworth, Middlesex: Penguin, 1948 [1927].

——. *O England!* London: Hamish Hamilton, 1934.

——. "The Plight of the Farmer" [letter to the editor]. *The Spectator* 29 Aug. 1931.

——. *The Professor on Paws*. London: Collins, 1926.

——. "The Right to Kill." *The Democrat* 30 Dec. 1922.

[——.] "To Evadne." *Grand Magazine* Sept. 1913.

——. *The Wintringham Mystery*. Serial *Daily Mirror* 1 March–6 April, 1926. Revised as *Cicely Disappears*.

Iles, Francis. *As for the Woman*. New York: Doubleday, 1939.

——. *Before the Fact: A Murder Story for Ladies*. London: Gollancz, 1931. Revised edition, London: Pan, 1958.

——. "Close Season in Polchester." In *Parody Party*. Ed. Leonard Russell. London: Hutchinson, 1936.

——. "Dark Journey." In *To the Queen's Taste*. Ed. Ellery Queen. London: Faber, 1949.

——. "Eastern Love Song." In *Press Gang: Crazy World Chronicle* Ed. Leonard Russell. London: Hutchinson, 1937.

——. "It Takes Two to Make a Hero." *Saturday Book 3*. London: Hutchinson, 1943. Revised as "The Coward." *Ellery Queen's Mystery Magazine* Jan. 1953.

——. "The Lost Diary of Th*m*s A. Ed*s*n." *Saturday Book 6*. London: Hutchinson, 1946.

——. *Malice Aforethought: The Story of a Commonplace Crime*. London: Gollancz, 1931.

——. "Outside the Law." *Strand* July 1934.

——. "Mrs Rattenbury." *Strand* May 1943.

——. "Rewards and Reviewers" [letter to the editor]. *Time and Tide* 21 March 1936.

——. "Was Crippen a Murderer?" In *Great Unsolved Crimes*. London: Hutchinson, 1938.

Platts, A. Monmouth *Cicely Disappears*. Revised version of *The Wintringham Mystery*. London: John Long, 1927.

ABC's Contributions to Detection Club Collaborations

Berkeley, Anthony. "Clearing Up the Mess." In *The Floating Admiral*. London: Hodder & Stoughton, 1931.

——. "In the Aspidistra." In *Behind the Screen*. London: Gollancz, 1983 [1930].

——. Lord Peter's Privy Counsel." In *Ask a Policeman*. New York: Berkley, 1983 [1933].

——. "The Policeman Only Taps Once." In *Six Against the Yard*. New York: Berkley, 1989 [1936].

——. "Tracing Tracey" and "Bond Street or Broad Street?" In *The Scoop*. London: Gollancz, 1983 [1931].

Iles, Francis. "The Rattenbury Case." In *The Anatomy of Murder*. London: Bodley Head, 1936. Reprinted in *More Anatomy of Murder*. New York: Berkley, 1990.

Secondary Sources

Newspapers and Periodicals Consulted Extensively

Book Review Digest 1927–40

Daily Telegraph 1933–36, 1971

The Humorist 1923–26

John O'London's Weekly 1938–39
London Opinion 1924–25
Manchester Guardian 1938–39, 1956–71
New York Times 1927, 1931, 1933–34, 1939
The Passing Show 1922–26
Punch 1922–29
Saturday Review 1931–32, 1939
Sunday Times 1952–56, 1971
Time and Tide 1932–33, 1936
Times 1928, 1937, 1971
Times Literary Supplement 1926–28, 1930–33, 1935, 1978
Tit-Bits 1923–25

Books and Articles

Barnard, Robert. "The English Detective Story." In *Whodunit? A Guide to Crime, Suspense and Spy Fiction.* Ed. H.R.F. Keating. New York: Van Nostrand, 1982.

——. *A Talent to Deceive: An Appreciation of Agatha Christie.* London: Collins, 1980.

Barnes, Melvyn. "Anthony Berkeley." In *Twentieth Century Crime and Mystery Writers.* Ed. John Reilly. 2nd ed. New York: St Martin's Press, 1985.

Barzun, Jacques, and Wendell Hertig Taylor. *A Catalogue of Crime.* New York: Harper & Row, 1971.

Bourgeau, Art. *The Mystery Lover's Companion.* New York: Crown, 1986.

Breen, Jon L. *What about Murder? (1981–1991): A Guide to Books about Mystery and Detective Fiction.* Metuchen: Scarecrow Press, 1993.

Carr, John Dickson. "The Jury Box." *Ellery Queen's Mystery Magazine* July 1972.

Christie, Agatha. *Partners in Crime.* London: Fontana, 1958 [1929].

Cooper, John, and B.A. Pike. *Detective Fiction: The Collector's Guide.* Taunton: Barn Owl Books, 1988.

Dale, Alzina Stone, and Barbara Sloan Hendershott. *Mystery Reader's Walking Guide to London.* London: Sphere Books, 1987.

Desmond, Ray. *Dictionary of British and Irish Botanists and Horticulturalists, including Plant Collectors, Flower Painters and Garden Designers.* Revised edition. London: Natural History Museum, 1994.

Fletcher, J.S. "The Maybrick Trial." In *Great Unsolved Crimes*. London: Hutchinson, 1938.

Graves, Robert, and Alan Hodge. *The Long Weekend: A Social History of Great Britain, 1918–1939*. London: Cardinal, 1985 [1940].

Greene, Doug. "Yet Another Note on the Least-known Member of the Detection Club (and Some Others)." *Crime and Detective Stories* 12 Nov. 1989.

Haycraft, Howard. "Anthony Berkeley Cox." *Wilson Library Bulletin* 14 Dec. 1939.

——. *Murder for Pleasure: The Life and Times of the Detective Story*. New York: Carroll & Graf, 1941.

Iles, Sybil M. *The School of Life: A Study in the Discipline of Circumstance*. London: Elliot Stock, 1905.

Johns, Ayresome. *The Anthony Berkeley Cox Files: Notes towards a Bibliography*. London: Ferret Fantasy, 1993.

Keating, H.R.F. *Crime and Mystery: The 100 Best Books*. London: Xanadu, 1987.

Morgan, Janet. *Agatha Christie: A Biography*. London: Collins, 1984.

Moy, Paul R. "A Bibliography of the Works of Anthony Berkeley Cox (Francis Iles)." *Armchair Detective* 14.3, 1981.

Panek, LeRoy Lad. *An Introduction to the Detective Story*. Bowling Green, Ohio: Bowling Green State University Popular Press, 1987.

——. *Watteau's Shepherds: The Detective Novel in Britain, 1914–1940*. Bowling Green, Ohio: Bowling Green State University Popular Press, 1979.

Philmore, R. "Inquest on Detective Stories." Part 2. *Discovery* Sept. 1938.

Queen, Ellery. *In the Queen's Parlour and Other Leaves from the Editor's Notebook*. London: Gollancz, 1957.

——, ed. *101 Year's Entertainment: The Great Detective Stories, 1841–1941*. Boston: Little, Brown, 1941.

Robyns, Gwen. *The Mystery of Agatha Christie*. New York: Doubleday, 1978.

Sayers, Dorothy L. *Have His Carcase*. London: Gollancz, 1932.

——. *The Letters of Dorothy L. Sayers 1899–1936: The Making of a Detective Novelist*. Ed. Barbara Reynolds. London: Hodder & Stoughton, 1995.

——, ed. *Great Stories of Detection, Mystery and Horror*. 1st, 2nd and 3rd Series. London: Gollancz, 1928, 1931 and 1934.

——, ed. *Tales of Detection*. London: Dent, 1936.

The Sherborne Register 1550–1950. 4th edition. Sherborne College, n.d.

Shibuk, Charles. "Anthony Berkeley." In *Dictionary of Literary Biography* 77. Detroit: Gale Research, 1989.

Steinbrenner, Chris, and Otto Penzler, eds. *Encyclopaedia of Mystery and Detection.* New York: McGraw-Hill, 1976.

Strickland, William Bradley. "Anthony Berkeley Cox." In *Twelve Englishmen of Mystery.* Ed. Earl F. Bargainnier. Bowling Green, Ohio: Bowling Green State University Popular Press, 1984.

Symons, Julian. *Bloody Murder: From the Detective Story to the Crime Novel. A History.* Harmondsworth, Middlesex: Penguin, 1974.

Turnbull, M.J. "The Wonderfully Fallible Roger Sheringham." *Clues: A Journal of Detection* 17.2, 1996.

——. *Victoria History of the Counties of England: Hertfordshire.* Vol. 2. London: St Catherine's Press, 1923.

Wilson, Colin, and Patricia Pitman. *Encyclopaedia of Murder.* New York: Putnam, 1962.

Wynne, Nancy Blue. *An Agatha Christie Chronology.* New York: Ace Books, 1976.

Ziegler, Philip. *King Edward VIII: The Official Biography.* London: Collins, 1990.

Index